Urban Hinterlands

Urban Hinterlands

Planting the Gospel in Uncool Places

Sean Benesh

White Blackbird
BOOKS

About White Blackbird Books

White blackbirds are extremely rare, but they are real. They are blackbirds that have turned white over the years as their feathers have come in and out over and over again. They are a redemptive picture of something you would never expect to see but that has slowly come into existence over time.

There is plenty of hurt and brokenness in the world. There is the hopelessness that comes in the midst of lost jobs, lost health, lost homes, lost marriages, lost children, lost parents, lost dreams, loss.

But there also are many white blackbirds. There are healed marriages, children who come home, friends who are reconciled. There are hurts healed, children fostered and adopted, communities restored. Some would call these events entirely natural, but really they are unexpected miracles.

The books in this series are not commentaries, nor are they crammed with unique insights. They are a collage of biblical truth applied to current times and places. The authors share their poverty and trust the Lord to use their words to strengthen and encourage his people.

May this series help you in your quest to know Christ as he is found in the Gospel through the Scriptures. May you look for and even expect the rare white blackbirds of God's redemption through Christ in your midst. May you be thankful when you look down and see your feathers have turned. May you also rejoice when you see that others have been unexpectedly transformed by Jesus.

Other books in the White Blackbird Book series:

*Heal Us, Emmanuel: A Call for Racial Reconciliation,
     Representation, and Unity in the Church*
Everything Is Meaningless? Ecclesiastes
The Organized Pastor
Birth of Joy: Philippians

Praise for Urban Hinterlands

With soaring house prices in all the cool cities, especially the one I'm from, Vancouver, BC, Benesh anticipates a rise in church planting in between these central city neighborhoods and the manicured suburbs. Read this book if you're discerning where God is calling you to plant. Perhaps you'll end up in a place that you never thought you would.

Daniel Im, coauthor of *Planting Missional Churches*, director of church multiplication at NewChurches.com, and teaching pastor at The Fellowship

By 2050, nearly 70 percent of the world's population will live in cities—urban, suburban, and in between. In *Urban Hinterlands* Benesh starts a crucial conversation about the role and relationship of the church in this new frontier—how does the church serve the whole city, not just the cool or comfortable parts, and in a way that creates common good without disrupting and displacing? If you're comfortable with being part of this larger conversation without needing all the answers, this will be a book that challenges and pushes you to think about planting and pastoring in ways you probably haven't before!

Zach Yentzer, Curator, 100 Creative Cities

Table of Contents

Foreword by Alan Briggs xi
Introduction xv

Chapter 1   Living in an Uncool City 1

Chapter 2   Transitions 11

Chapter 3   On the Quest for Livability 21

Chapter 4   Place and Identity 29

Chapter 5   The Cost of Livability 37

Chapter 6   Wrestling with the Gospel 47

Chapter 7   What is Truly Livable? 57

Chapter 8   Keeping Cities Gritty 67

Chapter 9   What Do We Really Want? 77

Chapter 10   Loving Uncool Places 85

Afterword 91
Bibliography 92
About the Author 93

Foreword

If you've never visited Phoenix in the winter, you need to. Seventy degrees for Christmas is surreal. It's a triple espresso shot for the frozen soul. What many people don't know about Phoenix is that it sits just a two-hour drive below tall pines in chilly air with incredible vistas. From these mountain roads, you could put your car in neutral and ride the brakes the whole way down to the warm (or in the summer, burning) valley of the sun.

I love the tall pines and mountain trails of Payson and Flagstaff that remind me of my own Colorado mountains. I also love the palm trees and pools in the desert below. Both have a mystique and offer many reasons to reside there. One time while coasting down the winding road I had this thought: people actually live between these beautiful mountains and the desert floor. They reside in "the space between," the part between the tall pines and the palm trees.

This is a book for those who live between the proverbial valleys and mountains. Perhaps your town or neighborhood isn't new enough, historic enough, beautiful enough, or hyped up enough through social media posts. Just like the mundane nature of most moments in our lives, most places are not something to write home about. They get overlooked by the edgy neighborhoods, the cultural hubs, and the cities that reek of utopia. Sean Benesh and I share a common love for these in-between spaces. There is great Kingdom potential that has not been realized in many dots on the map, no allure that has magnetized the creatives or the affluent. Denominations haven't targeted them, and church planters aren't flocking there. Perhaps Gospel networks that developed years ago in Denver, Austin, or Seattle have not been conceived yet in your place. Perhaps your place has a low self-esteem from being left out by the cool kids.

In my role as a church planting catalyst and equipper of missional misfits, I help people process one of the biggest decisions humans face: where to live. I often meet with people or teams who are chasing "the right place" to plant their lives and sow the Gospel. I walk them through misnomers and opportunities about various places. I am no longer surprised when these folks pass over my city looking for something hipper, hotter, fresher, more family-friendly, or simply more likable than my place.

I resonate with this book because I happen to live in one of those "barely on the radar" in-between places. Just like every place on the face of the earth, there are rips in the fabric of my city that you would never know about if you didn't inhabit it for awhile. There are also great opportunities.

It is equal parts exciting and heartbreaking to listen to conversations about place within the church today. Some are asking how they serve the cracks in their neighborhoods. Many are tackling issues their local newspapers perpetually cover. Church communities commonly relocate their ministry hubs to growing areas of town where their parishioners live. Pastors are struggling to believe that a long season of small-town ministry equates to faithfulness. Seminarians look for roles at cutting-edge churches in urban centers that serve better coffee than their grandparents' churches. Benesh is one of a few prophetic voices asking us to reconsider where we choose to live and, perhaps, how we choose to engage in the mundane place we find ourselves.

We live amid an intense pressure for everything in our lives to be impressive and Instagram-worthy. Unfortunately, that has come to include where we live and serve. It's as if we need to justify the place we live and serve based on how needy, pagan, cultured, growing, or post-everything it is. That leaves most places feeling like they're the last kid picked for the kickball game behind the school.

Location mattered enough to Jesus to settle into the mundane places and spaces. Incarnation was Jesus's ministry model; his silver bullet was coming and living among us, amid gritty humanity. If you have been questioned about the validity of life in your place, you're not alone. Jesus took heat about the place he was from. In the first chapter of John, Nathanael asked, "*Can anything good come out of Nazareth?*" (John 1:46). Unknowingly we ask the same questions Nathanael did. Why would God want me to go to Cedar Rapids? What impact could I possibly make in Bismarck? Could anything be worthy of my time in Topeka? Why not head to influential places like Denver, Austin, or Seattle?

In *Urban Hinterlands*, Benesh pokes the bubble of "cool" so we can see the need and the opportunity in the oft-neglected places. Whether your place seems "hipster cool," boring, or gritty, Benesh offers appropriate and timely confessions and conversation for those brave enough to pull up a chair. He pushes us to reexamine our commitment and imagination about the place we currently reside or the next place we will choose. This is a crucial book for anyone with a desire to put Gospel seeds in real, local soil. Read this book as warning, encouragement, and challenge to inform how you view your place.

Alan Briggs
Church planting catalyst, parish pastor, author of *Staying is the New Going: Choosing to Love Where God Places You*

Introduction

This book is full of personal confessions. Most of those confessions are related to selfish motives that are subterranean in ministry. We all have them, but rarely are we honest enough to admit and confess them. I feel like I'm an honest person. Frankly, I find it quite easy to be honest with *others*; the person with whom I'm the least honest is *myself*.

I tell myself all kinds of absurdities. When applied to a ministry setting, these can become even more troublesome if they're hidden behind the veneer of what I assert to be God's leading. For me, it is easy to confuse my deepest desires with what I sense God is saying and where he is leading.

But I'm fine with that. If we all waited around until we're absolutely satisfied our motives are pure, then we'd never do anything. We'd be stuck. Paralyzed. Unable to move forward and pursue God.

This book is essentially about motives. What motivates us to start churches where we do? I know every church planter says "God told me" to plant in such-and-such a place. If that were true—and I get into that in the book—then God must not care about uncool places, because most planters are *not* starting churches there.

As I said, this book is about motives.

My intention is not to question your calling or your walk with God. Instead, I want to invite you into a deeper wrestling between calling and wants. And this is where my personal confessions come to light. I struggle with this, too. Will you give yourself permission to be honest with yourself?

Here is my first confession. While I write on the need to plant the Gospel and new churches in uncool places, I do so from probably the coolest place in the United States: Portland, Oregon. Double-minded. Speaking from both sides of my mouth. Guilty as charged. But I also want you to know that places like Portland don't light my fires for ministry. They're too cool. Too perfect. Too well put-together. I love places with more baggage.

So here we are, on the front end of this journey together. Let's make a pact. Let's be honest with each other and with ourselves.

Ready?

Chapter 1

Living in an Uncool City

When we look back, we often can trace key moments that were formative in setting the trajectory of our lives. These powerful experiences shaped us in profound ways. This could be a memorable experience on a lake with your father at 5:30 a.m. that set in motion a love for fishing; or stumbling across a jazz concert in the basement of a nondescript venue in New York City that was formative in your passion for this musical genre; or a friend dragging you up a mountain summit on a hike on a June morning in the desert that captivated you enough that your life now revolves around trekking through the wilderness alone or with friends or family; or a bicycle ride through downtown from coffee shop to food cart that instilled a love for urban cycling.

Sometimes these events are pleasant experiences and produce nostalgia. Other times they are forced upon us, like losing a parent at a young age, growing up in a war-torn country, or coping with a long-term illness or disability. We simply would not be who we are without them.

When I was in college, I remember hearing a Chuck Swindoll sermon about some of the most brilliant and transformative figures in modern history. Each of them had faced extreme hardships and adversity. Through great adversity and tragedy, their character and resolve were solidified.

Sitting in a coffee shop in Portland, Oregon, I am mindful of the experiences that have shaped my own life. An ACL surgery my freshman year in college was transformative for me because all I could do post-surgery between physical therapy sessions was lie around and do homework. It was the first time I had ever earned a 4.0 in my life! I had previously never thought of myself as particularly smart or adept in school, but that experience changed me, and I didn't have another B the rest of college. It stirred within me a love for academics, school, reading, and writing.

Another experience that set the trajectory of my life was when right after starting seminary, my wife was hospitalized to treat bipolar disorder. Before that, neither of us knew or thought much about mental illness. After that, we often dealt with the reality of trying to mitigate its negative extremes. Numerous hospitalizations, 9-1-1 calls, police and paramedics visits to our house, and 2:00 a.m. trips to the emergency room regularly remind us how this has profoundly shaped our lives, how we make decisions, and our firm commitment to a loving and healthy marriage relationship.

Perhaps it's because I have a bohemian flare—I started college as an art major—but I love concepts, ideas, and places that are off the beaten path. Not only that, but in my love for sports this means I enjoy following teams and conferences that not many people talk about. For example, in the early 1990s I became a huge fan of the Boise State football team, long before they had their magical run of successful BCS or top bowl games, including their memorable win over Oklahoma in the 2007 Fiesta Bowl. Today I am a fan of teams like New Mexico State, Southern Utah University, and Idaho State. Even last night I took my youngest son to a college basketball game featuring two small colleges you probably have never heard of. For me, it was just as much fun as going to see major college hoops or the NBA.

This mindset has crept into my love for cities that are largely unknown and not top-tier. A few weeks ago, I was walking the streets of Quebec City, a place considered off the beaten path by many in the US (even though it is touristy), which is precisely why I enjoy visiting there. However, one of the most transformative experiences for me was moving to the off-the-beaten-path city of Tucson, Arizona.

I admit that when my wife and I were considering moving to Tucson I visited there to get the lay of the land ... and I hated the city. I literally was sick to my stomach thinking of moving there. It was not pleasant, not pretty, and nothing close to desirable. As we drove through the city, there was a knot in my stomach, especially driving along Speedway Boulevard through midtown. I was sickened to think what life would be like in that city. Luckily (or unluckily) we found a place in a distant suburb that was palatable and made the move seem more reasonable. So we moved.

What I didn't know then was that I would fall absolutely in love with this city that still to this day is sprawling, gritty, and rough. Speedway Boulevard is still as ugly as the first time I drove down it.

When we arrived in Tucson I decided to adopt an attitude I had learned in college from a conversation I had in passing with another student. I grew up in small-town Iowa and found myself going to college in inner-city Omaha, Nebraska. I didn't enjoy the experience, disliked the city, and couldn't wait to get out. But one day this student who had come from the far reaches of northern Minnesota said, "You know, there has to be a reason why so many people live in this city. I am going to explore it and find out why." That attitude became formative in how I approached Tucson. I didn't like it, love it, or understand it, but I figured that while I was there I should find out why a million people lived there and what made the city unique.

At first, it was easy for me to explore *everything but* Tucson. The endless wilderness and mountain ranges that punctuate the southeastern Arizona horizon beckoned me to explore. I trekked through alpine meadows 10,000 feet up in the Pinaleño Mountains, boulder-hopped at Cochise Stronghold in the Dragoon Mountains, took sledding trips atop the Santa Catalina Mountains at Mt. Lemmon, and explored mining towns like Hayden and San Manuel north of Tucson. But over time my heart and love eventually, miraculously, became deeply moved for the city itself.

That love has never left. When I had been gone six years, I had no idea how emotional it would be for me to go back. I cried like a baby as I drove around and retraced the steps of our lives there. It wasn't the tear-trickling-down-the-cheek kind of crying that guys are known for, but it was the full-on snot-bubble convulsive crying that accompanies deep anguish. I was shocked, alarmed, and deeply shaken by that show of emotion. Ask my family. I never cry. So what was it? What was it about the city that elicited such deep and raw emotion?

Then I remembered that it wasn't the first time I had wept over Tucson. What came flooding back were all the years I spent pining, longing, and pleading to the Lord on behalf of the city. I had spent much time prayer-walking in places overlooking the city while I was both a church planter and a church planting strategist. All I could think and pray about was to see this city transformed by the Gospel. There were places I recall walking, with the city stretching out below, where I pleaded before the Lord to see a church planting movement take place.

Tucson is certainly not cool by any stretch. Sure, there have been changes around the downtown and University of Arizona areas, but by and large the city still remains the same ... gritty, ugly, and all that is bad about urban sprawl and urban planning that prioritized the automobile over every other form of transportation. But it doesn't matter to me. I love that city *in spite of* how other people think of it.

Cities and people are a lot alike. Most of us live with deep-seated insecurities, and we do our best to mask them. Like applying makeup to cover a blemish, we curate the right kind of image to portray on social media. We highlight the positives and for the most part resist giving into the full range of our emotions, frustrations, and struggles online. Sure, there are enough people out there who seem to have left their filters in the third grade when it comes to verbalizing internal dialogue, but most of us are cautious. We simply want to put our best foot forward. We seek to control our image and in a sense brand who we are to the watching world.

Cities are no different. There is a sense among "lesser" cities that they either need to work hard to overhaul their image or fashion one that is loosely based in reality. Tourism magazines most often make cities more desirable and livable than they really are. It is the same as the nerdy girl living next door to the popular girl who is the high school homecoming queen. Our insecurities are only accentuated when we compare ourselves with others. When it comes to branding and curating the right image, cities are slaves to this as well. When living in Tucson, I realized how uncool and unsexy the city was when I visited other cities like Seattle or Portland or San Francisco. Usually if people found out I lived in Tucson their response sounded to me like, "Ah, how cute. What a pleasant little town for old people to vacation at in the winter." But like the parent of that nerdy girl, I didn't really care how cool other places were or what other people thought ... I *loved* Tucson.

I am old enough now to realize how things tend to turn golden over time. We gloss over pain and adversity in our past or at least make them out to have been less painful than they really were. Something in our brains doesn't seem to allow us to relive the intensity of struggles or at least smoothes over how unpleasant things really were. It is like growing up in small-town Iowa. In my mind as a child it was a substantially sized town that took awhile to trek across. Distances were enormous. However, whenever I go back to visit every few years, I am immediately struck by how small it really is.

So when I returned to Tucson and began driving toward downtown, I remember thinking, "Wow, this really is a gritty and raw city!" I had forgotten. My golden memories quickly vanished, and I was instead confronted with an untamed,

Western, pioneer, gritty, unkempt, sprawling desert city close to the Mexican border. But it didn't really matter to me.

I loved and still love Tucson.

Maybe you can relate. Maybe your city just isn't that cool. Sure, through gentrification and downtown redevelopment projects many central cities are trekking toward earning that "cool" moniker, but your city just isn't that cool yet. Maybe in another ten years when your streetcar is operating, there are ample trendy eateries, and a more robust bicycle infrastructure you will find that those highly coveted Millennials are arriving in droves and building your city's reputation as cool and trendy, but you're just not there yet. Maybe you live in Las Cruces, New Mexico, or El Paso, Texas, or Waterloo, Iowa, or Oklahoma City, Oklahoma, or Springfield, Illinois, or Cheyenne, Wyoming, or Waco, Texas, and while there are signs of hope and movement in the direction of cool, you still have decades of an uncool label hanging over you.

Rest assured. You're in a good place. I have been to the *other side* ... and you're not missing anything.

Here's the caveat, though. It is easy for me to type that last paragraph as I sit in Coava, the over-the-top trendy coffee shop on Hawthorne Boulevard in Portland, surrounded by a sea of hipsters. The decor and the quality of the coffee are second to none. I admit I have the luxury of planning my day around which trendy coffee shop I will make my office or writing place. There are simply too many options, and so to make life easy I've reduced it to only a select few like Coava or Heart. I remember before moving to Portland that my only option was to choke down Starbucks coffee. But even on my most recent visit to Tucson I noticed how the city has turned a corner as far as coffee with Presta, Cartel, and Exo all roasting amazing coffee.

Again, what do you do if your city is uncool? Or maybe we should reduce the scale. What do you do if your neighborhood or part of the city is not cool? Yes, Portland *is* trendy and cool, *but* that is reflective of life *inside* the city. Once you leave the central city, you will find we have ample strip malls, enormous arterials, and both urban and suburban sprawl even despite our urban growth boundary. Our suburbs are just like your suburbs.

What I am concerned with and think about constantly pertains to doing ministry and more specifically church planting in these kinds of uncool places. If you look at city after city, it is usually the safe and family-friendly suburbs or hip and trendy urban neighborhoods to which most church planters are "called." That's to say, for some strange reason God only seems to call people to plant churches and their lives in parts of the city that rank high in livability, and in the case of the urban districts, to those with abundant urban amenities.

But what do you do if that is not you? What if for some strange and glorious reason you buck the trend and plant your lives in an uncool city and in a gritty neighborhood that doesn't elicit any notion or emotion of civic pride? The kinds of places where you mutter under your breath to people outside of that city or neighborhood that you actually live there. And not only that, but the people you minister among are not fashionable. They may drive old pickup trucks, speak a foreign language, show up at Walmart at 11:30 p.m. with a toddler wearing only a diaper, still listen to '80s heavy metal music.

8

Maybe you've gone to seminary to become a pastor, and your contemporaries have gone on to find sweet gigs in the suburbs with congregations full of well-to-do people who drive nice cars and are polite. Instead, you've become the pastor of a church that was started in the '50s in an anonymous neighborhood. It's not that it's a rough neighborhood, but it's neither urban cool nor suburban safe, just somewhere in between. The address says it is within the city limits. The church building hasn't been updated since the late 1970s, the congregation is cantankerous and has run out the last two pastors, and the average age continues to grow older. But you're there. You see the neighborhood full of other declining '50s-era housing stock and strip malls that are uglier than the day they were haphazardly thrown together to make a quick profit.

These kinds of places are what I call the *urban hinterlands*. The *in-between* places between trendy central city neighborhoods and manicured suburbs. The basis of my framework and the place that forms much of my imagery is Tucson. Sorry, Tucson.

My last visit there earlier this month found me doing multiple driving tours around the city. Driving down Speedway Boulevard again was a reminder of how uncool this city is. A stop at a restaurant along the way revealed a room full of uncool people. From pedestrians (what little there were) to those I observed as I traversed midtown Tucson continued to remind me that this is no Portland.

Maybe you live in a gritty, unkempt, and uncool city or neighborhood, and this all is a painful reminder that there are no trendy eateries or coffee shops in your neighborhood. Rest assured. This book is about you and *for* you. I am *with* you.

While cool cities like Portland or San Francisco or Manhattan continue to garner the attention and imagination of church planters across the country, this book is about giving love and attention to the *other* places. Having lived in Portland for several years now I have lost track of all the coffees I've had with visiting prospective church planters and core teams looking to plant here. The city continues to attract young educated Millennials. As the national (and international) media fawns over Portland, it has attracted a bumper crop of church planters.

But *your* city is not and has not seen this overflow of church planters and people wanting to plant churches and their lives there. Frankly, and unspiritually speaking, it is simply because your city is not cool enough. Again, I know, because I left a city like your city to go to a cooler place.

Chapter 2
Transitions

I vividly recall when our children were younger that I didn't want them growing up in Tucson. That is difficult to admit. In my mind, I wanted our boys to have more "options" in life, and I feared they'd be "stuck" in Tucson with little economic opportunities unless they joined the military or made missiles. By that time I was drinking the Richard Florida Kool-Aid about the creative class, urban amenities, and how and why cities are attracting a glut of young creatives. Since I didn't see that happening in Tucson, I decided I wanted to be somewhere that it was.

I had (and have) a love / hate relationship with Tucson (as you've seen by now). I love the city, its gritty funk and rawness, but at the same time the more I traveled to other cities the more I realized how good other cities had it. When I'd visit cities on the West Coast like San Francisco or Seattle, I would be dumbfounded by all of the young creatives that had collected there sipping coffee in Third Wave coffee shops, riding Fixies, or pecking away on their MacBook Pro computers, launching some cool new business. I would salivate over the proliferation of urban amenities, the urban sophistication found in the city center, the livable streets, the creative artisan economy, bicycles used for transportation, and so much more. Over time I began dreading the flight back to Tucson.

I decided I had to get out.

I told you this book was about personal confessions.

I even began working on a degree in a non-residential program that was based in downtown Seattle. I would fly up there for one to two weeks at a time. My life was immersed in that city, walking all over the place, exploring new sites, eating seafood along the waterfront, and seeing what a creative and economically vibrant city was all about. This elevated my angst for Tucson. Again, I dreaded the flight home.

When I worked as a hiking and mountain biking guide, I would be out on the trail each day for hours with affluent guests from big cities like Manhattan, Chicago, or San Francisco. Almost all were CEOs, high-powered executives, business owners, and the like who lived in the city center. I'd hear stories of what life was like living in these big cities, tales of car-free lifestyles, eating Chinese take-out at the corner store, and their love for the pulsating rhythms of big city life. Sure, Tucson was considered a big city compared to where I grew up in small-town Iowa, but I would always leave those conversations feeling as if I were missing out on something.

During four-hour group hikes we would talk ... *a lot*. We would share stories, family backgrounds, career aspirations. Initially, I would beam with pride about living in Tucson. But repeatedly the globetrotting big-city dwellers would say some variation of the following about Tucson, "Yeah, Tucson is a great place to *visit*, but I could *never* live here. It is too small and doesn't have much to offer me." I thought that was absurd. How could one *not* like Tucson?

The overall impression from countless conversations was that Tucson was a sleepy little sprawling city that wasn't really a "big boy" city. It didn't have the density and amenities that these people had grown accustomed to. At first in my mind I was dismissive of these painful comments, because I simply couldn't see what they were talking about. I was convinced they had become numb to *really living* by having lost themselves in the crazy, consumptive, and hectic lifestyle found in big cities. *They* were wrong, and *I* was right. But as I transitioned away from being a hiking and mountain biking guide to focusing more on being a church planting strategist everything began changing.

As I studied Tucson I also studied other cities to see what makes some cities more appealing than others. Why did some cities see cultural creatives moving there *en masse* while other cities saw these same people leaving? It was through this that I soon discovered how uncool Tucson was. Not only that, but also the struggles it had to diversify economically away from military and education (public schools, University of Arizona). Conversely, when I went to other large cities, I saw a whole new world ... an urban playground that I wanted to be part of, a lifestyle I was eager to try out and adopt, and to have access to more amenities than I knew what to do with.

And so we moved.

Now we live in Portland.

And yes, all of the stereotypes are true.

Before, while living in Tucson, when I would travel to other cities I sometimes was embarrassed to tell people where

I was from. As I mentioned previously, when people found out I was from Tucson they usually replied in the same way an adult responds to a child who built a lousy display at the science fair. The child is told (in a feeling-sorry kind of way) that his project was better than it actually was. But he *knew* it wasn't that special and saw through people's attempts to convince him otherwise. But then I moved to Portland.

Now when I travel and people hear that I'm from Portland, the whole narrative changes. It is met with ooohs and aaahs. I became the kid who designed the cool volcano at the science fair that actually worked. Then the conversation is about how they desperately want to visit Portland, or move to Portland, or tell me about a fabulous trip they had vacationing there. I guess living in Portland makes you the cool kid on the block. It doesn't matter where I go, even among other really cool cities ... Montreal, Vancouver, San Francisco, or Brooklyn, there is always a nod of approval that I am a "Portlander."

I'm sure it is that same feeling when the uncool junior higher gets invited into the elusive and exclusive "cool kid club." Now all of a sudden there is a newfound power, a swagger in the step, and a new identity. Whereas a week ago that junior high girl or boy was marginal at best and riddled with insecurities, now he or she walks boldly and proudly through the halls with head held high, chin up, and chest out, and with a confidence that was missing last week.

So what is it like to live in not only a cool city but in the cool and hip inner city?

In church planting circles outside of the Pacific Northwest we were all fed a steady diet of how "dark" and "pagan" it is here. I heard these stories, as if people were talking about the 10/40 window in North Africa or the Middle East, of the need for church planting in places like Vancouver, Seattle, Portland, or San Francisco. As I looked around in Tucson it *felt* and *looked* and *was* unchurched in many ways. Most notably was that in a city of a million there were maybe one or two churches that crested two thousand people on a Sunday. But the Northwest was portrayed as the last frontier in church planting in North America. Paganopolis. Supposedly it was like spiritual anarchy here with the pagan population of Portland offering child sacrifices to unknown deities and drinking blood in Satanic religious rituals.

Actually, that's all a myth. Good marketing by denominations and church planting organizations trying to garner more funding and attract more church planters. Pretty slick.

One of the first things I noticed when I moved to the Pacific Northwest was the *strong presence* of the church and evangelicals here. I am not claiming it is the Bible Belt or anything like that. But I was utterly shocked and amazed at all of the mega-churches in the metro Portland area. Not only that, but the central city, like I mentioned earlier, has been a hotbed for new churches over the last few years. As these neighborhoods become gentrified and cool, it means more church planters are coming who were fed this belief of how dark Portland is and are moving here in droves to "push back the darkness" or "penetrate lostness."

But God has been at work here for a long time.

One of the go-to lines I have heard about the Northwest goes something like this: "The Pacific Northwest is not *post-Christian* ... you see, it is *never-was-Christian*." The image evoked is one of anarchy, debauchery, and rampant atheism. Not true.

Not long ago I taught an undergraduate course called History of the American City. It was pretty straightforward, and in it we gave particular attention to the history of Portland. As a result, I pored over the history of the city and region from pre-European times, to how and where the city was formed and founded, and what decisions and movements shaped the city. Yes, it was a frontier town with its share of rough lumberjacks, but there were a lot of people who moved here in the early days from more culturally savvy parts of the country, too.

Also, from the beginning there were always strong and active churches in the city. The notion of Portland and the Northwest being never-was-Christian makes for good marketing, but it is a myth. God has been at work in Portland from the beginning. The church has had its hand in caring for the least and the last from the beginning.

Today, because we are so cool, we are experiencing a glut of young college-educated Millennials. They are moving here in droves. I meet them all the time. They move from Nashville, Atlanta, Louisville, Dallas, Raleigh, Greenville, Kansas City, Omaha, Iowa City, Chicago. What do these places all have in common? They're all conservative Midwest and Southern cities. Sure, there is also a parallel storyline of people intentionally leaving these places and opting for the more liberal Portland. But there are *a lot* of people with Jesus and church in their backgrounds.

Ironically, as I was typing these words at one of my favorite local coffee roasters, I walked up to get a refill, and since I know where the twenty-something barista is from I pointblank asked her why she moved to Portland. The answer? To experience the culture of Portland, and the political climate was much more liberal than the conservative city and state she came from.

You see, when you're a cool city that has a growing national and international reputation for being a hotspot, people want to move there. Another common storyline, and one that Richard Florida attests to in his research, is that people decide to move to Portland specifically because it is cool as defined by the kinds of urban amenities and lifestyle that appeal to cultural creatives. Another tidbit that Florida highlights is how people move first and *then* look for a job. It used to be the other way around. People would move to places because they had found a job. More and more people are deciding where they want to live and then either finding a job or starting a company. I've seen it repeatedly.

A couple weeks ago, I was teaching these principles in an Understanding the City class for North Portland Bible College. One of the students, an associate pastor, exclaimed, "Hey! I just saw that today! I was sitting in a coffee shop, and this young woman sat next to me. We chatted, and she said that she *just got off the plane* from Boston. She moved to Portland not knowing anyone and had no job, but she wanted to come here and experience what life was all about here. If she didn't find a job, she was going to start a fashion company.

She asked me if I knew of any hostels or people looking for roommates. This is CRAZY!"

Welcome to Portland. This is what happens when you live in a cool city.

Now let me back up the truck for a moment. For the past thirteen-plus years my life has been defined by church planting and my involvement within this subset of ministry. This ranged from being a church planter myself to being a church planting strategist to teaching seminary classes at several different schools to writing books about church planting. Sure, I also write about bicycles, gentrification, high-density cities, and the like, but my heart and focus is predominantly on church planting.

Currently my ministry centers around training urban church planters and equipping them to do ministry in the city. *That is why I am writing this book.* I am a friend of church planters, and most of the people I meet in the course of a week are church planters. I love church planters and missionaries. I have given my life to the spread of the Gospel.

Yes, church planters are being drawn to cool cities and cool neighborhoods within cities. I get that. I affirm that. We need *more*, not less. I am not railing against the impact of neighborhood succession and the need to plant churches in places in the city that are either growing (suburban fringe) or gentrifying. I am not and will not shame people about the decisions they make on the *where* of church planting. I wrote this book because the cool places keep getting more and more church planters, whereas uncool cities and uncool neighborhoods still lag behind. We need more people willing to plant churches in the uncool places.

Why are we drawn to plant mostly in cool places?

I'd be a hypocrite to say I am immune to these push-and-pull factors, because that is precisely why I am living in Portland. It *is* cool. And do you know what? I *like* it here.

I also know full well the dynamic that shapes where we live and plant churches. As I mentioned previously, when I first encountered Tucson, I almost vomited in my mouth. It was gross and unappealing. However, once we checked out Oro Valley, a nice new suburb, I could envision living there. Was that vanity? Is that the same dynamic that influenced us moving to Portland?

How do we reconcile our never-ending appetite to live in vibrant, happening, and cool places? Are we simply seeking the pleasure that gratifies our flesh, which stands in opposition to the Gospel? Or are we following how God has hardwired each one of us?

I've actually met many church planters who *do not* plant in cool places. That leads me to believe that not everyone wants to live in inner-city Portland, Wicker Park in Chicago, Williamsburg in Brooklyn, or SOMA in San Francisco. Frankly, more church planters actually do plant in uncool parts of the city or simply uncool cities. So where is the rub?

I have said and taught for years that we self-select where we live based on cultural capability. What that means is that we most often move to places, whether a city or a neighborhood within a city, precisely *because* it resonates with who we are. For every person moving into the central city of Portland, there are three or four who land in the suburbs. These people view Portland with suspicious disdain and remark to their friends, "I just don't get Portland. It's weird."

Bill Bishop in his book *The Big Sort* gets at the heart of this, "As Americans have moved over the past three decades, they have clustered in communities of sameness, among people with similar ways of life, beliefs, and, in the end, politics."[1] What that means, as Bishop throughout his book contends, is that when people move they land in neighborhoods and cities that resonate with the value systems that are reflected and embodied in the neighborhood. In other words, we move to neighborhoods and cities among people who are *just like us.*

Am I in Portland basically because I am wired for affinity with the city? Is it because I am artistic, creative, casual, and thrive in creative, walkable, bikeable, outdoorsy, and liberal cities? Yes, it would seem so. Then the follow-up question is: Did God make me this way? Am I hardwired by the sovereign hand of God to think and value certain things that are reflective of how he knit me together? Could this explain why I am living in a cool city like Portland? Could this also explain why you are in your city whether it is cool or not?

And what do you do when you don't have a choice? What do you do when God tells you to plant your life, the Gospel, and churches in an uncool city?

---

[1] Bill Bishop, *The Big Sort: Why the Clustering of Like-Minded America is Tearing Us Apart* (New York: Mariner Books, 2009), 5.

Chapter 3

On the Quest for Livability

My time in the raw, dirty, and sprawling city of Tucson left me desirous of something *more*. This more could be summed up in one word: livable. What exactly is "livable" and why didn't I think of Tucson as livable? I mean, I *did* live there. But livable is not the same as *inhabitable*.

Sure, Tucson is not the most hospitable place on the planet. It has a million people living in a valley hemmed in by mountains. It is a community that gets its water from a depleting aquifer underneath the city or from the Central Arizona Project, which diverts water from the Colorado River. Open canals carry water to Tucson across vast stretches of open desolate desert. These canals, plus air conditioning, have made Tucson inhabitable by modern standards.

But in my mind, Tucson wasn't really livable. I know that my suburban experience clouded my judgment. As much as Portland is lauded for its livability, I'm sure those who live in its far-flung suburbs do not experience that reality. In the same way, my life in the sprawling, car-dependent suburbs of Tucson affected my outlook. Even then, the central city was not that dense or offer a robust walkable urbanism. It didn't matter to me, because I wanted to live in a livable city. Tucson was not it. I wanted out.

Admittedly, the term "livable" can be ambiguous. Some cite a diverse local economy, while others claim it is about aesthetic beauty in the built environment. Still others note the presence of a progressive political climate, low crime rates, positive health statistics, and so on. So what is livable and why was it one of the impetuses for me to leave Tucson in search of a hipper and happier city? What were my motives?

Making decisions based upon livability, while natural and innocent, can actually be dark and insidious. I say that as I look into the inner recesses of my own heart. Last week I began reading *In the Company of the Poor* by Dr. Paul Farmer and Father Gustavo Gutiérrez. Like a spotlight searing the cobwebs of my heart, working through this book has been both liberating and painful. It was not only a painful reminder of the reality of mixed motives, but it has been a clarion call to continue to die to self for the sake of the Gospel.

In the chapter titled "Conversion," Gutiérrez writes, "As a conversion is a break with sin it will have to have *both* a personal and a social dimension."[1] Our call to Christ is not only personal, but there is also a social dimension. It begins transforming us on the inside and that then spills into every other area of our lives—our relationships, how we treat others, our finances, how we live in our neighborhoods. But does it then also influence *where* we live?

Earlier in the book, Father Gutiérrez states:

---

[1] Paul Farmer and Gustavo Gutiérrez, *In the Company of the Poor: Conversations with Dr. Paul Farmer and Fr. Gustavo Gutiérrez* (Maryknoll: Orbis Books, 2013), 74. Italics mine.

> I do theology as one who comes from a context of deep poverty, and thus for me, the first question of theology is *how do we say to the poor: God loves you?* I understand that the words "God loves you" are not difficult to say. But this message—as true as it is—presents a monumental challenge given the daily life of poor persons and their experience of exclusion and nonlove, of being forgotten, of having no social rights .... And so, what does it mean to take seriously the question of how to say and to show persons living in the structure of violence, living in social injustice and seeming insignificance, that "God loves you?"[2]

Framing livability with that mindset as the backdrop changes the entire conversation. Most often, when we talk about livability the focus is on what *we* are getting out of it. Cities are amenities to be consumed. However, when the lens of the Gospel is applied, the narrative decisively shifts to what we will *give*. Christ died for us. He *gave* himself so that we can give ourselves. Jesus said, "As the Father has sent me, even so I am sending you."[3]

But I didn't always see it that way.

When I visited Portland, I saw bicyclists everywhere, sleek streetcars moving about the city, a plethora of hipsters and creatives sipping on lattes or brews, and a dense, walkable, and vibrant urban core. There was a buzz and electricity in the city. The large flywheel of momentum was carrying the city forward to further national and international prominence. I

---

[2] Ibid., 27.

[3] John 20:21.

had to live here and experience what the buzz was about. This was certainly a livable city, I thought.

So I left the sprawling sunbelt city of Tucson for the Pacific Northwest. My family immersed ourselves in our new home city of Portland. Not only did we move to the city, but we moved into the inner city, where all of the magic takes place. When I was in Tucson I had found *one* coffee shop that was worthy of the Pacific Northwest. That's because the owner/roaster had moved from Seattle to start the shop, and I had to drive twelve miles to get there. But in Portland? Multiply that same shop by forty, add a dozen, and hipsterfy it, and you'll see what kind of city I live in.

Portland is *livable.*

But livability is more than having an ample number of coffee shops or local craft breweries. The small city blocks, robust number of cultural creatives, and multiple forms of transportation make up the perfect *container* for these different facets of livability and create the fertile soil for them to grow.

This week I am in the Near Southside neighborhood of Fort Worth, Texas. I am meeting with business owners, church planters, urban planners, and nonprofit leaders in preparation for a Gentrification Studio I am facilitating. The Near Southside is redeveloping (and slowly gentrifying) to try to become a more "livable" and inviting urban neighborhood on the southern flank of the central business district.

Shortly after I arrived for my first meeting, someone handed me a brochure called *A Guide to Fort Worth's Near Southside.* Inside the front cover it reads:

Nestled among many of Fort Worth's oldest and most distinctive neighborhoods, the Near Southside is easily accessible from anywhere within DFW, with proximity to major highways I-30 and I-35 as well as the TRE commuter rail system. Featuring an infrastructure designed with pedestrians and cyclists in mind, the vibrant urban district defies expectations—eclectic neighborhoods uniting with creative businesses to engender collaborative approaches to community.

Located centrally, the Near Southside is positioned near many of Fort Worth's most popular destinations—Downtown, Sundance Square, the Cultural District and TCU. Hosting an assortment of destinations and landmarks, as well as events drawing crowds year-round, the district's truest currency is the definitive sense of place bestowing commercial endeavors and creative institutions with their own style.

Sounds appealing, doesn't it? So if we read between the lines of creative branding and marketing, we see that the area has been *unlivable* for decades due to downward cycles of disinvestment, neglect, and population dispersement. Through the use of Tax Increment Financing, much-needed money is being reinvested into the Near Southside. For what purpose? To make it livable.

In Fort Worth, I saw encouraging signs of things trending toward urban renewal and repopulation. Again, the key ideology present is livability. This neighborhood is the next in a long line of places pushing to become desirable, which in the end means livable. Or is it the other way around?

Many of us are on a quest for the elusive meaning of livability. Central city neighborhoods were abandoned in previous generations as people found livability on the urban periphery ... suburbia. However, the tide has turned, and now livability is synonymous with urban cool, and we are flocking *en masse* back into central city neighborhoods. This has been and is my story. From finding and defining livability in the suburbs, now I find myself living and enjoying the urban amenities that a livable city offers. If there were a quest for a livable city, then I have found it. Quest complete. Game over. Put me out to pasture. But is my hometown of Portland *really* livable? That is a question and conversation for another chapter. For now, back to the quest.

Consuming Livability

If we are honest, livability as we have come to mean it boils down to a lifestyle not only to partake in, but to consume wholeheartedly. Since moving to Portland I have been swallowing this lifestyle hook, line, and sinker. I live in a very walkable urban neighborhood. I have both a Whole Foods *and* a Trader Joe's two blocks away. I live above a coffee shop, four blocks from a light rail station. I bicycle all over the city, sipping on locally roasted coffee (and roasting my own). When I need a bike part at 9:50 p.m. I walk across the street to Velo Cult and pick up what I need.

But I have noticed something insidious growing in my heart ... complacency, apathy, and an overall neglect for the least and the last. Sure, there are dozens of homeless people we see daily in our neighborhood, but that is about the extent of the struggle we see. Walk out into the parking lot of our building, and you'll see numerous German auto imports from Mercedes to BMWs. Just across the street from our four-story building (which is hemmed in on either side by other four-to-five-story apartments) you'll quickly leave urban density for early twentieth-century single-family homes. Their hefty price tags mean that only those with deep pockets could afford to live there. Apart from the homeless population in the neighborhood who have simply become background noise and visual texture, the area continues to grow in affluence and livability.

So I have found a livable city and a livable neighborhood, which means the quest is over, right? Isn't that the title of this chapter, "On the Quest for Livability?" I've found it. I am here. I am living the dream. It is not only me, but also the thousands of cultural refugees who've made the transition to embrace, experiment with, and consume the lifestyle in the same way we did. After awhile everyone is wearing plaid, drinking locally roasted coffee and beers, and launching their own artisan start-ups, myself included.

But is my quest for livability truly over? Am I left for the rest of my life to attempt to fit into skinnier jeans, attend latte art competitions for baristas, and keep writing books in coffee shops? Is this nirvana? Utopia? No, it is just Portland ... but I am not convinced it is as livable as the city's branding and marketing would lead you to believe. In fact, the longer I am here the more *unlivable* it feels ... and then my attention, mental wanderings, and heart turn back to Tucson.

Urban Hinterlands

Chapter 4
Place and Identity

I remember telling my wife that when I turned thirty I wanted to get a head start on my midlife crisis so I could get it out of the way. I got real radical and bought a mountain bike (I actually assembled a used one with mismatched components) and several years after that I picked up a $750 moped. My midlife crisis was averted, and I moved back into the domestic duties of being a dad and breadwinner. It was a close call.

Throughout my thirties and now into my forties, I think about identity a lot. Since I'm not open enough to have these conversations with others, I end up with a continuous inner dialogue in my head, which only reinforces my insecurities. Interestingly, though, the tide of my identity seems to rise and fall not only with what I am doing in life, but more importantly (which gets at the heart of this book) on *where* I live. Same guy, same everything, but labels and geography play a key role.

Place shapes our identity.

We can argue about how this is shallow and self-centered thinking that only reinforces insecurity, but it is still there.

While I know I am shaped by the Gospel and that I am the aroma of Christ to God, I am still influenced by my environment.

Our identity is directly influenced and impacted by place.

When I travel, I sense a certain gravitas when I say I am from Portland. People don't really know I grew up in small-town Iowa. There are perceptions about people who are from Iowa, and there are perceptions about people who are from Portland. One diminishes your social standing, while the other gives you kudos. Particularly since I'm passionate about biking, when I say "I'm from Portland," people listen. I'm the same guy I was in Iowa or Tucson, but if I tried to sell those ideas without the Portland label, I don't know that anyone would buy them.

Unfortunately in ministry or church planting circles, the conversation is the same. As I've said more times than I can remember, all of the cool cities or cool spots in the city are on the receiving end of a glut of church planters. Yet we continue to shy away from uncool cities and uncool parts of the city. Do you mean I should plant a church among uncool people? People who don't get my fashion, who don't get my sophisticated music tastes, who don't get my fine coffee or beer palette, or who generally don't get my chic urbanite leanings? You mean plant a church among *those*? Those people who drink Folgers, pound Miller Lites, drive beat-up pickup trucks, shop for clothes at Walmart, listen to country music, and are not educated? Why would anyone throw away life to plant a church in *those* cities and in *those* neighborhoods?

If we find our identity in living in cool places, we will keep planting churches in the neighborhoods where we bump into many other cool church planters in the same coffee shop. It is not uncommon for me to hear of two, three, or four church planters *all* planting in the same cool neighborhood. While each came unaware of the others, they are planting their denominational flags into the soil of this trendy neighborhood (or one that's transitioning into a trendy district). If we want to address this trend, then we need to peel back the layers and get into the heart of things, namely our identity.

Identity and Calling

More honesty. Often authors write about topics that either they are interested in or wrestling with. If one were to read all my books in one sitting, there is little doubt that along with my passion for understanding the city, the shaping influence of the built environment and transportation infrastructure, and church planting in urban contexts, there are other subplots woven throughout. Calling is a topic I constantly pick up, polish, and put back down.

This past week I picked up the book *Vocation: Discerning Our Callings in Life* by Douglas J. Schuurman. To say that I devoured it would be an understatement. In a matter of a few days I not only had read the book, but I had dog-eared, underlined, starred, and written on a countless number of pages. The book jolted and jarred my thinking. Perfect timing for this chapter.

Not long ago I was asked what prompted me to be an author. Ironically I don't consider myself an author, nor do I brandish that term to identify myself (even though I've written nine books to date). My response to this church planter was probably more uninspiring than helpful. I simply replied that I write to wrestle. I write to learn. I write to hammer out intriguing concepts. I write to uncover more depth on topics I want to learn about. Sometimes I enter into a writing project with only vague ideas of where I want to go and no idea the route to even take to get there. That's why calling resurfaces in many of my books.

Calling is a subject that haunts me. Perhaps it haunts you, too. Not haunt in a doom-and-gloom sense, but rather in the sense that I want to make sure I'm not only living a life worth living, but doing so for the glory of God, the furtherance of the Gospel, and the flourishing of humanity. I want to "get it right."

Schuurman addresses the modern assumptions about calling that are not only deceptive, but have an enormous pull and influence on the *where* of church planting in the city. "A related modern assumption is that to have a calling is to experience self-fulfillment in that calling. A job is a way to get a paycheck, but a vocation is more than that; it is a realm of self-fulfillment."[1] When we reduce calling to a sense of self-fulfillment, why would anyone in his right mind ever think of planting a church in an uncool city or uncool neighborhood? It is to this end that Schuurman continues, "It is not fulfillment of the self but the glory of God and the welfare of the neighbor that ought to determine 'vocational' choices, insofar as there is room for choice. In and through one's vocation one picks up one's cross, follows Christ, and participates in his

---

[1] Douglas J. Schuurman, *Vocation: Discerning Our Callings In Life* (Grand Rapids: William B. Eerdmans Publishing Company, 2004), 117.

self-sacrificial sufferings. Christians should not aim at self-fulfillment."[2]

This is not an attempt to browbeat us into overlooking or neglecting how God wired us, how we grew up, the influence of our environment, our DNA, personality, or giftings. But it is an attempt to push back against an *Americanized* version of that calling that seeks self-gratification and comfort. Let's be honest. Why don't church planters want to plant in unassuming neighborhoods? There are lots of reasons. Bad schools, unsightly streetscapes, too many pawnshops and check-cashing businesses, neighborhood instability, and depreciating home values. One push in past decades for many church planters landing in the family-friendly suburbs was good schools and family security.

I've had these kinds of conversations with a number of church planters. In their minds why would God call them to parts of the city where the schools were average or underperforming? Why would God call them to parts of the city where they may not be able to have a slice of the American dream (a single-family detached home with a big yard for the kids)? Why would God call them to the parts of the city where there are many lower-income families? Certainly God would not call planters there. Besides, it may negatively impact their image as a pastor.

Admittedly I am being a little harsh. But you see, we *all* have these kinds of internal conversations. We all do. We're just too embarrassed to admit it. It's okay. I am with you. But I've also made the plunge. I did the unthinkable before my

---

[2] Ibid., 118.

family landed in Portland. We sold our suburban home with four bedrooms and a massive two-car garage. We moved into an urban neighborhood in Vancouver, BC, where most kids didn't speak English. Out of the fifty schools in the district, ours ranked forty-seventh. Third from the bottom. We moved into a tiny apartment. We walked and used public transit exclusively.

Do you want to know what hurt the most? My identity. It messed with me. Shopping at the Dollar Tree for groceries and getting all of our clothes at the thrift store was not cool or trendy. It was hard. Yet it was what it was. We survived. We made it. We grew. We learned. We loved it. Best thing that could have happened to us. Changed everything about how I view cities, live in them, and experience them.

On the flip side I am *not* saying that everyone should go and do likewise. That would be foolish. This is descriptive and not prescriptive. My goal is not to shame you into moving to uncool cities or uncool neighborhoods. I am simply pleading with you to have an honest conversation with yourself.

The funny thing about internal dialogue is that you actually can be brutally honest. Weigh all the variables and alternatives. If you opt for the burbs or a cool gentrified neighborhood, then to God be the glory. But if you're motivated by cool, then maybe you need to hit the pause button and think things through more.

Again, Dr. Schuurman says:

> All pivotal decisions should be shaped by a sense of calling, by our desire to express gratitude to God for the gift of salvation by using our gifts to serve others

and glorify God. This includes career decisions, decisions relating to marriage and family, decisions to join this or that church community, and various other major commitments to voluntary organizations. All of these should be motivated by *gratitude* toward God and directed by *freedom* working in love to serve God and our neighbors. The call to be a Christian must govern all decisions about callings. Pivotal decisions, like decisions within one's callings, ought to be guided by love, shaped by shalom, and tested by discernment.[3]

The goal then is that our lives become so radically shaped by the Gospel and what God thinks of us that place has little bearing on our identity. Then we will discover the freedom, motivated by gratitude, to wholeheartedly love the least and the last around us.

---

[3] Ibid., 130.

Chapter 5

The Cost of Livability

Sometimes I am perplexed by my own dichotomies. I am like that spoiled kid who received everything he wanted for Christmas only to be soon bored with it all. Unsatisfied. Discontent. Wanting more.

In many ways I wanted Portland, and I got what I wanted. Like a Christmas present pulled out from under the tree on Christmas morning, I shredded the wrapping paper and behold ... *the gift*. Just what I always wanted. Portland.

Then came the dreaded discovery ... some assembly required, or not all parts included, or go online to purchase upgrades. In essence, the gift was going to cost me *a lot* more than I realized. It is like paying $45 for a new video game only to realize that you have to pay for a yearly online subscription and regular expansion packs. After a year, that $45 game has cost you about $135.

This is what it feels like living in an alluring city. The nice apartment we moved into four years ago was affordable *then* (barely). But our neighborhood has become much cooler since then. Within three blocks there are six coffee shops, three pubs, a Whole Foods, a Trader Joe's, and several mixed-use developments. The result? Rent prices have *soared*.

Just last week I had a conversation on the elevator with one of our neighbors who lives a couple doors down. She has been in the building since it was built thirteen years ago. She said the first ten years rent increases were minimal at best, but in the past three years the rate hikes have increased dramatically.

We're being priced out.

Everything we loved and desired about this neighborhood is going by the wayside. Untouchable. Well, only touchable for those who can afford it.

Our lease is up in a few months. We're weighing the options for what to do next. Leave now? Six months from now? Try to squeeze out one more year? I have extra adjunct professor gigs lined up to give us a cushion, but after that it is anyone's guess.

Over the weekend, I spent a few hours scouring the Internet for rentals in this part of the city in our price range. When I entered our specifications, there were virtually *no* listings in the entire core of Portland. Nothing. There are plenty of places to rent, but not in our price range. So we had to zoom the map out quite a bit. *Way* out.

I recently saw an infographic that explained the leap in rental prices in Portland. Six years ago the average rent price in Portland was very reasonable. Six years ago. Now? Doubled.

Cool has a lofty price tag. As Portland continues to garner national attention and cultural creatives move here in droves, supply cannot keep up with demand. The cooler the city, the more people who want to live there, which means it becomes more expensive ... and exclusive.

Referring back to the map and our rental search, the correlation is obvious:

Cool = expensive
Less cool = affordable

If we wanted to leave the magic of Portland's city center, we most certainly could find something more affordable. But we'd have to live quite a bit farther out. Also, since we now have one vehicle and our kids are locked into schools in the heart of the city, what does that mean? Change schools? Drive a lot?

See? I told you I sounded like the spoiled kid at Christmas. Wanting something—or *someplace*—like Portland, and now that I have it I'm complaining that it is not satisfying. I suppose I want to have my cake and eat it too.

This is how "pioneer" gentrifiers felt. Decades ago impoverished bohemians and artists moved into central city neighborhoods. Why? Because it was affordable as well as close and accessible to urban amenities. But people weren't moving into these neighborhoods in droves. Instead, those who could, whether White or Black, were moving out to safer neighborhoods with better housing and schools. Those who couldn't afford to move—or minorities to whom developers and realtors refused to sell homes—were stuck in the urban core. Redlining by banks only exacerbated these conditions, and urban neighborhoods spiraled downward.

When these bohemians moved in they did so because they could actually afford it. Sure, many also enjoyed access to the city and the "grittiness" of urban life compared to the burbs, but the bottom line was that it was affordable. These *were* the urban hinterlands.

But the landscape changed. When a growing number of artists and other cultural creatives began collecting *en masse,* they began rebranding the neighborhood. A few studios, galleries, and new eateries later, and all of a sudden the neighborhood appears to be "on the rebound." That attracts more people and more investment.

So the next wave of gentrifiers typically has money. They can afford to buy straight out, invest in the homes, encourage the banks by their presence to stop redlining, and the reputation of the neighborhood begins to change.

Then the third wave hits. People with even *more* money move in. Amenities were already coming in, but this next wave prompted more exclusive ones. Instead of a grocery store, it was a Whole Foods. Instead of a soul food diner, it was a high-end New Orleans bistro. Ironically, the pioneer gentrifiers then start being priced out. If they were renters, they can no longer afford the neighborhood that was once affordable to them. The original gentrifiers suffer the effects of gentrification.

Metro Vancouver, BC, is another case in point. An article by a Canadian research group, the Angus Reid Institute, says, "With housing prices soaring higher than the peaks of the North Shore mountains and the transportation issues of a growing region on the ground, will a generation of more than

150,000 families simply leave Metro Vancouver in search of more manageable living?"[1] The article also says:

- Eight-in-ten (79 percent) say high housing costs are hurting Metro Vancouver; just 9 percent say they're beneficial.
- Nearly nine-in-ten (87 percent) are worried that the next generation won't be able to afford a home here.[2]

Apparently the housing crunch in Vancouver is even worse than in Portland. I actually lived in Vancouver for several years, too, and know how it is often held up as a bastion of good urban living, sustainability, multiculturalism, and smart growth. It is a breathtakingly beautiful city. The downtown peninsula is sophisticated, cool, clean, walkable, bikeable and has great public transit, ocean and mountain views, and plenty of amenities including an enormous world-class urban park.

But livability equals expensive. Again, the simple math is that the cooler and more desirable the city, the more expensive it becomes. The Angus Reid Institute article mentioned above concludes by noting:

> Most Metro Vancouver residents anticipate a bleak future if the housing status quo in the region continues. While some groups are better situated to benefit from

---

[1] Angus Reid Institute. "Lotusland Blues: One-in-five Metro Vancouverites experience extreme housing & traffic pain; most of them think of leaving." *Angus Reid Institute.* Online: http://angusreid.org/vancouver-real-estate/, para. 1.

[2] Ibid., para. 6-7.

the current state of affairs, it appears every segment of the population believes that the younger generation is being disenfranchised, and that the majority of residents would like to be a part of the solution.[3]

If cities like Vancouver, Seattle, Portland, and San Francisco continue to see their costs of living skyrocket, the brands of their cities may be helped but their general populations will be hurt. As a result, I believe the "lesser" cities will then be on the receiving end. In other words, young migratory cultural creatives will eventually find other cities that are not quite so cool ... and expensive. Cities like Tucson or El Paso or Albuquerque are incredibly affordable and may soon become the new places to be.

Now before you think Portland will stop being Portland and people will leave in droves, turning Portland into a post-apocalyptic wasteland, not so fast. Desirable cities like Portland will always be desirable, but especially for younger generations and cash-strapped start-ups, they may just not be suitable nor livable.

That then begs the question: What is livable?

If you're starting up a new company (or church) and you don't have a lot of money, why would you want to be in a city where you have to pay exorbitant home and office rental prices? For some businesses it does make sense to cluster with others in the same industry. If you're into bikes—making bicycles, components, and accessories—then it certainly makes sense to live in Portland. But at what point will enough be

---

[3] Ibid., para. 71.

enough and cash-strapped start-ups begin clustering in other more affordable cities?

Recently a local article in the *Willamette Week* summarized much of the angst about Portland's growing lack of affordability, which is tied to its growing cool reputation. The article details the construction of the Burnside 26, a new chic mixed-use apartment building in the inner city. The angst is over how new projects like this are reflective of the "new" Portland, and how the city's transformation is causing longstanding residents much frustration and concern. Writer Tyler Hurst said:

> The heart of these complaints is change. People want a city that's great to live in, so more people want to live there. Neighborhoods morph, property values go up, rents climb, and a minimum-wage earner can no longer afford a one- or two-bedroom apartment close to downtown or the Willamette River. It's even more acute here, where the urban growth boundary ringing Portland encourages residential density.
>
> Every city has been through this change. It's heartbreaking, painful, and not fair. It's not fair that people with money can come in and change a neighborhood. It's not fair that longtime renters have no say in how the property they call home is maintained or sold. It's not fair that wages have been stagnant for years. It's not fair that the people who helped make Portland awesome are now being pushed farther away because outsiders see how great this place is. It's not fair at all.
>
> Nor is it fair to love a city and not want to share it.[4]

---

[4] Hurst, Tyler. "Why My Apartment is Good for Portland." *Willamette Weekly*, June 9, 2015. Online: http://www.wweek.com/portland/article-24869-why_my_apartment_is_good_for_portland.html, para. 38-40.

There it is. When many of us scratch and claw our way to livable cities, in the end our efforts make these desirable cities unlivable. We got all that we wanted. Then we flipped the price tag over and ... *gasp.*

But this book is not simply about what is or is not livable and the cost to live in such a place. This book is about church planting in seemingly *unlivable* places. Again, those could be the "lesser-tiered" cities or even neighborhoods within the "cool" cities. While church planters are bumping up against one another in the central city, a ten-minute drive, bike ride, or bus ride east, and the whole scenario changes. Drastically.

From urban cool to a true urban hinterland that is neither trendy urban nor suburban safe. In Portland, 82nd is the dividing line. Everything east rapidly becomes more ethnically and culturally diverse, lower income, and affordable (i.e., less "livable"). Everything west, toward downtown, becomes whiter, more affluent, and expensive (i.e., more "livable"). West of 82nd and in the central city is where the vast majority of new church plants are here. East of 82nd are very few church planters.

So why is livability the determining factor for *where* most of the new churches are being planted? In our call to follow the countercultural nature of the Gospel, shouldn't it be the exact opposite? I have acknowledged my own double-mindedness in this area. My desire is that all who proclaim the Gospel would be mindful of this cultural tendency so we may fight against it.

No doubt, what is deemed livable comes at a cost. However, it is more than the cost of what it takes a church planter to live in these kinds of places and plant a church, it comes at even a greater cost of those places—the urban hinterlands—that are continually neglected and left off the radar of many church planters, denominations, and church planting organizations. I see on a weekly basis how these same people and church planting entities continue to target exceptional cities (i.e., livable) to plant new churches. In North America that means San Francisco, Chicago, Raleigh. Internationally it means Dubai, London, Zurich. But where does that leave places like Bakersfield, California, or Nairobi, Kenya?

This conversation needs to be coupled with digging into population migration trends. We frequently hear that "more than 50 percent of the earth's population now lives in the city." For many that means there should be a greater emphasis on cities like New York, Los Angeles, Paris, Tokyo. However, where these new city dwellers live is something we are not paying close enough attention to.

> The world's population of 3.3 billion is unevenly distributed among urban settlements of different sizes. 52 percent of the world's urban population resides in cities and towns of less than 500,000 people ... Despite the attention they command, megacities—cities with over 10 million people—are home to only 9 percent of the world's urban population.[5]

In the United States the trend is similar. "A greater proportion of the urban population resides in agglomerations of less than 5 million people, with small-sized cities of less

---

[5] UN-Habitat, *Planning Sustainable Cities: Global Report on Human Settlements 2009*. London: Earthscan, 2009, 27.

than 500,000 accounting for 37 percent of the urban population."[6] That means the vast majority of Americans live in what I am calling the urban hinterlands. They live in Globe, Arizona, and Socorro, New Mexico, and Medford, Oregon, and Marshalltown, Iowa. And yet most current church planting strategies seem to bypass any notion of these urban hinterlands—where the majority of Americans live—and go straight to large, affluent, expensive, and "livable" cities.

---

[6] Ibid., 28.

Chapter 6

Wrestling with the Gospel

I've already shared about my first trip back to Tucson after a six-year absence. Since then I've been back a few more times. I am about to go back there again. In light of struggling with Portland's affordability, my hidden and deep-seated love for Tucson, plus Tucson's endless sunshine and the fact that I can mountain bike there 365 days a year, I'm afraid of where my mind will go when I'm back. And since we're on a short-term lease in Portland, will I be tempted to jump ship and move back?

In Tucson, we could easily buy a house, cut our housing budget in half, and make our income stretch *a lot* further. My ministry role is not dependent on any particular location, so that is not tying me to Portland. But our kids trump any decision to move. With two in high school and one starting in a year, it would be foolish to uproot them. Also, two of our boys are fanatical skaters, and Portland is *the spot* for skateboarding. They often skate with pros at one of the local skateparks or run into them while working out at our gym.

So what then is at the root of this deep-seated longing for Tucson? I believe it is the longing for home. Why do I call a city I lived in for only six years home and not small-town Iowa where I grew up? Several reasons. It is where I fell in love with cities. It is where I fell in love with God's call to be involved in church planting. It is where my wife and I began raising our boys. It is where I fell in love with mountain biking. It is where I fell in love with a city that I prayed and wept over. There's an inexplicable emotional bond there. Home.

But it can also be a dangerous longing. Nostalgia is powerful yet deceptive as Timothy Keller explains in *The Prodigal God:*

> "Home" exercises a powerful influence over human life. Foreign-born Americans spend billions annually to visit the communities in which they were born. Children who never find a place where they feel they belong carry an incapacity for attachment into their adult lives. Many of us have fond memories of times, people, and places where we felt we were truly home. However, if we ever have the opportunity to get back to the places we remember so fondly, we are usually disappointed.[1]

That well describes how I felt on my first visit back to Tucson. I am worried those will be my emotions again when I return.

I don't want to be dismissive of attachment to place. In our hyper-mobile society, we certainly need a course correction for our lack of connection to place, to home. As the conversation of localism continues to pick up inside and

---

[1] Keller, Timothy. *The Prodigal God: Recovering the Heart of the Christian Faith.* New York: Riverhead, 2008, 102.

outside the church, it is having an enormously positive impact on our neighborhoods, churches, and cities.

But I do want to be critical of the longing that revolves around curated memories and relationships no longer rooted in that place. It is the same in regards to the homes we grew up in and our memories as a child. As much as I identify Tama, Iowa, as the place where I grew up, living in the same house for the first eighteen years of my life, it is not the same. It can never be the same. Most of my childhood friends grew up and moved away, and the house I grew up in is owned and lived in by someone else. If I were to move back there, it would only be with a dim reflection of what I knew and experienced of that place.

Keller goes on to write, "Home, then, is a powerful but elusive concept. The strong feelings that surround it reveal some deep longing within us for a place that absolutely fits and suits us, where we can be, or perhaps find, our true selves."[2]

We are longing for a world, a *true* home, that isn't tainted by sin. "In the beginning of the book of Genesis we learn the reason why all people feel like exiles, like we aren't really home."[3] Since Genesis 3 we have all become exiles of sorts. Longing for home but never really finding it. Never fully having arrived regardless of how much we love and embrace the city in which we dwell. This is not predicated on the city's coolness or lack thereof. We can be home, but not fully.

So when I visit Tucson and revisit memorable spots, I want to feel the tug of my heart and let the emotions come.

---

[2] Ibid., 103.

[3] Ibid., 107.

But at the same time, I want my emotions to serve as a reminder that I am an exile. Even if I move back to Tucson, I would not be truly *home*. Once God purges the world of sin and decay and sets things right, then and only then will my longings be realized.

Our deepest longings and desires (whether hidden or in the open) play an influential role in how we view our cities and their supposed livability. They also greatly impact *where* we plant churches. For most, it is easy to love, appreciate, and become emotionally attached to places that are deemed livable or cool.

However, I am wired the opposite.

I like off-the-beaten-path places, unpopular places, uncool places. I am quite content with obscurity. For that reason, I sometimes chafe at living in Portland. It is almost too cool for me. I'm withering. Because of that, I have periodic regrets about having left Tucson.

But when I was actually in Tucson last, I was surprised to find that the more I drove around, the less it felt like home. When I am away, the more it feels like home. The more I visit, the less it feels like home. I vividly recall driving through some neighborhoods in the urban core and being struck by the city's foreignness to me. I thought, do I *really* know this city? Or is it just that I've held on to select memories?

I asked myself then, do I *really* want to move back to Tucson? The answer was no. In other words, all the emotions and time spent reflecting on my decision to move *after* we left does not reflect the thought processes, decisions, motives, and why we decided to leave in the first place. When I'm away from Tucson, I second-guess myself. However, once I'm back and really immerse myself in the city, I remember why I left in the first place. That's not a slight to Tucson. I simply wanted opportunities that at the time it could not provide for me.

That last statement is unfortunately a common storyline for many who have moved to urban hinterland places only to leave a few years later. Since leaving Tucson I've been able to be an adjunct professor at three different seminaries and two colleges. I knew I had to leave Tucson to lean more into my desire to teach and be around students. Also, a couple of those teaching opportunities are precisely the kinds of places I want to teach in since they reflect incredible diversity among the student body.

Regrets and longing. I have regrets for sure. I also have a deep longing for Tucson and the type of city it is. I'm over Portland's pretentiousness. I'm tired of the storyline of cool when it comes to this city. I long for beat-up, uncool, and struggling cities. I know, this is my personality quirk. This is why I follow struggling, perennially losing football programs like New Mexico State. Not that I want them to stay bad, but to follow, track, and see what it takes to see them turn around. The same goes with cities. I am passionate about watching struggling cities turn around and reinvent themselves while keeping their DNA and identity in tact.

The longer I'm in Portland, the more I shun the over-the-top hipster image of the city. Instead I find myself longing for the uncool parts of the city, like east of I-205. More and more, these areas are becoming (or already are) minority neighborhoods. In a comforting way, I am reminded of Tucson.

I recently took my Bicycles, Equity, and Gentrification class from Warner Pacific College to east Portland to help out at Rosewood Bikes, a new nonprofit bike shop. Rosewood Bikes is being incubated in the Rosewood Initiative, which does community and economic development in the neighborhood around 162nd and Stark. This area houses the highest rates of crime, poverty, and single-parent families in the metro area.

The bike shop is the only one in a five-mile radius. It's not meant to be a hipster hangout selling single-speeds. It is meant to help people in the neighborhood get onto bikes so they can better access jobs and opportunities in the city. We spent the day stripping bikes of parts to either reuse or recycle. My students were introduced to the storyline of the neighborhood and why there is a need for a bike shop like this.

I think I have found a home and a people I can really get my arms around. Over the summer I brought my family out to this area a few times to play frisbee golf. Each time we'd show up to the park I'd notice that usually 80 to 90 percent of the people there were "visible minorities." This was a great feeling. I felt like I was home.

Wrestling with the Gospel

Emotions are powerful. They sway our decisions, often more than we realize or would like to admit. For church planters, too, emotions play a significant role in deciding where they will plant a church and their lives. Again, more than we realize or would like to admit.

We look for that spark or aha moment when exploring a city or neighborhood. Having introduced many church planters to new cities and neighborhoods, I am always mindful of that spark. When I was a church planting strategist in Tucson and would host potential church planters, I'd take time before they arrived trying to identify how God wired them, parts of the city that would be a good match, and neighborhoods in the city where there was the greatest need.

When church planters arrived, we would spend a day or two driving around the city, exploring, and talking. In essence, what we were looking for was that spark. Were they the result of powerful emotional responses? Spirit-led? Usually there was a combination of both. I am convinced that while at times our emotions can be deceiving and untrustworthy, they are also the vehicle God uses to move, prompt, and catapult us forward. We're not merely robots responding to data and logical equations.

Since there's a certain level of emotion intertwined with calling, church planters are compelled to love where they plant. When talking with planters, you hear them beam with pride. Maybe that is the crux of my disconnect with Portland. There was a calling—a compulsion—to move to Tucson to plant a church. In Portland we're simply "here." It makes an enormous difference.

With that said, what do we do about the reality that most uncool cities and neighborhoods are simply overlooked? If my story is at least a fraction of what could happen in the lives of other church planters, it reveals that God can give us a supernatural love to embrace and cherish the unlovable. I hesitate painting places like Tucson in this light because it certainly isn't based on what or how I feel about that city, but the perception to the outside world is that it is a bit gritty. But how many places, since they are left off the map of church planting strategies, are missing out on church planters who would fall head over heals in love with them despite their flaws, warts, and idiosyncrasies? Conversely, how many church planters miss out on being exposed to places where they would fall madly in love with and tangibly meet needs but are overlooked because the city doesn't have a veneer of cool.

Yesterday I spent the day with Alan Briggs. He is a friend who shares my love for off-the-beaten-path places. During the course of our five-hour bike tour and exploration of Portland, we talked much about places like his home city of Colorado Springs and surrounding communities like Pueblo. We both having a longing to see more churches planted in the urban hinterlands.

The Gospel continuously confronts our cultural syncretism. While we can easily identify forms of syncretism in other cultures, it is harder for us to see how we've succumbed to syncretism in our own culture. We have cultural blinders. I recently read about a large evangelical church removing their lead pastor for pride, arrogance, domineering leadership, and self-promotion. Syncretism with culture.

The point? We wrestle with culture daily. We are blinded to the numerous messages the world generically and our culture specifically communicates to us. We buy into the value system. Promote self. Look out for one's own good. Seek the path that will put you on top. Go the route of comfort. Buy into materialism and self-preservation. Or for church planters, plant churches in comfortable and livable settings.

But the Gospel confronts us in our syncretism and compels us to daily die to self as we wrestle with this good news that Christ calls us to abandon all for. The Kingdom of God as the pearl of great price or the buried treasure in the field is worth any amount of sacrifice (in this case, more like inconvenience) we may encounter. Christ laid it all on the line for us. He is the one who truly sacrificed everything. He counted our lives as more valuable than his own. His rescue mission required everything. We are to go and do likewise. It is time to wrestle more deeply with the Gospel and the implications it may have on where churches are planted. Maybe then we would see a bumper crop of more churches planted in the urban hinterlands.

Chapter 7
What is Truly Livable?

Earlier I asked: What is truly livable? After chewing on that question for a year, I am starting to gain some clarity. I am seeing that livable is really in the eyes of the beholder.

In the last chapter, I alluded to what kinds of cities and neighborhoods are appealing to me. But I know many people who would look at cities like Tucson, El Paso, or neighborhoods east of the 205 in Portland and say, "No thanks. Not on your life!" So this notion of livable is indeed nuanced.

Like most people, I go through phases. For awhile I had this over-the-top strong draw toward deeper academia. I began working on a second doctorate and found such joy in reading obscure academic journals and thick, dry textbooks. I was in the groove of reading, researching, writing, and talking about these topics nonstop. The amount of information I was consuming was like drinking out of a fire hose.

For awhile I loved it, but as time went on, it became too much. I noticed that my deep love for cities began fading. Everything became, well, academic. The love, curiosity, and wonder that I held for cities diminished. Soon it became simply another subject. My heart shriveled. I stopped caring. I stopped reading and stopped writing. Everything related to the city became a chore.

Simultaneously I became disillusioned with the city, with my city. While it had captivated my wonder and imagination, I felt like I was slowly being crushed under the weight of information while also struggling to live in this city that was rapidly becoming more and more unaffordable for my family. Counting down the days until we were going to be priced out was (and still is) causing anxiety. Where would we move? How far out would we have to drive to find something that was affordable? What are we going to do about the boys' schools?

So I unplugged.

Literally.

I stopped reading books, blogs, articles, and social media information related to cities. Instead I found myself packing up my mountain bike and heading into the mountains. I had had enough. I even began talking with my wife about moving to a small town, somewhere far enough away but not too far from an airport for when I fly out for work.

I was looking for an escape.

Portland, although lauded for its livability, was becoming crushingly unlivable. I wanted out.

Just yesterday in the *Oregonian* newspaper there were a few articles detailing Portland's growing lack of affordability. One of the articles was even titled "Working class priced out, kicked out in new Portland housing boom." It described the new "hipster hovels" (micro-unit apartments) in NW

Portland. Even though these units are only 250 square feet, they are still garnering incredibly high rent prices.

Jeff Manning, who wrote the article, said:

> The boom raises troubling issues of economic inequality, as rent hikes have spiraled far beyond workers' wage increases. The posh new apartment houses are prevalent on Portland's east side, historically the gritty home to the city's working class. Even developers share foreboding that the central city is becoming a playground for the affluent while the young and the old and the people in the service economy no longer can afford to live there.
>
> Critics have coined a nifty phrase for the trend—"economic apartheid."[1]

This article raises the question, too: What is truly livable?

In my Bicycles, Equity, and Gentrification class at Warner Pacific College, we recently spent the entire time discussing these topics and why inner-city Portland is at the forefront of the conversation. We talked about how what happens in one part of the city directly impacts other parts of the city. As housing prices in Portland's central city rapidly escalate, there continues to be a growing throng of people opting out.

Opting out is a kind way to put it. The first round of rising prices impacted the African American community in inner North and Northeast Portland. Many were priced out or

---

[1] Manning, Jeff. "Working class priced out, kicked out in new Portland housing boom." *The Oregonian*, September 22, 2015. Online: http://www.oregonlive.com/watchdog/index.ssf/2015/09/post_19.html, para. 8-9.

simply cashed out. The latest round of displacement is "White on White." We could say that the early gentrifiers are being gentrified themselves. There has been much media coverage of this phenomenon locally, but I don't have to read the paper to know about it. I'm watching it happen in my neighborhood.

According to some articles, people are not only opting to move east of the 205, they're simply leaving Portland altogether. Many were drawn to Portland over the last ten years because of its bohemian culture, livability, affordability, bikeability, and artisan economy. But that has also become a magnet for our recent real estate boom. Those who've come to experience Portland for being Portland are becoming alarmed that the charming Portland they "once knew" (all of five to ten years ago) has changed, and fast. Again, supply cannot keep pace with demand. In Real Estate 101 that means prices continue to skyrocket. That's why owners of apartments are able to charge whatever they want, because vacancies are practically nonexistent and there's a line to get in. As soon as one tenant is priced out, there are others to take the place at a higher price.

Is this *truly* a livable city?

I've lived life comfortably in the suburbs before (though it feels like a lifetime ago). With two gas-guzzling SUVs, we had our cookie-cutter home and car-dependent lifestyle. After that, we traded it all in to become "poor immigrants" in Vancouver, BC, where we simply struggled to live in our high-density urban neighborhood. All sense of living comfortably was jettisoned as the goal was to simply survive. Fast forward and now the luster of living in bohemian inner-city Portland has worn off as we're counting the days, reconfiguring our family budget, and seeing how long we can even make a go of it here. How many side jobs do I need to take on simply to live in Portland? That is a question I ask myself constantly.

But perspective is everything.

Sometimes I need to step outside of my own vantage point and view the city from the perspective of soon-to-be-residents. I had opportunity to do this just a few days ago. I occasionally lead downtown bike tours for visiting groups. Yesterday I took ten people who were visiting from San Diego out on a bike tour. More than simply visiting, they were here exploring the city, discerning the Lord's guidance, and making plans to move here in less than a year to begin the process of planting a church. This was the core team of a future church plant along with the church planter.

I have to be honest and admit that the ideas, topics, and rants from this chapter were echoing in my head as I pedaled downtown to meet up with them. Of course I strategically selected a hipster hangout coffee shop for us to meet. After introductions and giving an overview for our tour, we walked over to a bike shop to pick up our rental bikes.

Throughout our tour of Old Town/Chinatown, the Pearl, SW park blocks, PSU, and South Waterfront, I talked a lot about the hot topic of Portland's growing unaffordability. I also talked about gentrification, displaced minorities, and the working class. However, as the tour continued I felt my heart and attitude slowly change as I kept emphasizing Portland's commitment to different modes of transportation (e.g., light rail, streetcar, etc.) with a specific emphasis on our bikeability. I was wearing down my own defenses.

We happened to take a tour on a picture-perfect fall day in Portland—70 degrees, sunny, and with the leaves beginning to change. To compound the awesomeness, our bike tour route landed us smack in the middle of the route for Sunday Parkways. This is an event where a route through the city is closed down to cars and is only accessible by bicyclists and pedestrians. To make matters even *more* awesome was this also coincided with the recent opening of the Tilikum Crossing Bridge. This is not simply another new bridge across the Willamette River leading into downtown Portland, but it is completely *car-free*. The only modes of transportation on the bridge are light rail, streetcar, bus, bicycles, and walking.

By the time we reached the bridge, there were *thousands* of people on bikes or walking across the bridge. It was a spectacle to see. My out-of-town guests from San Diego had never seen anything like it. After we pedaled across to the east side and then back again to the west side of the river via the Hawthorne Bridge, we stopped and debriefed our entire bike tour.

They were truly amazed at how livable and accessible (transportation-wise) Portland was. While we did address life east of the 205 and the needs there, there is no denying that Portland is truly a livable city. I throw my hands up in agreement. I still have to sometimes pinch myself to realize I live in such a marvelous city. However, that does not mean there are not needs and problems at hand.

Which brings us to the tension. Yes, Portland is going through a real boom. As more and more people move here, it is increasingly becoming more expensive and unaffordable due to a housing shortage. That pushes many away from the city center where the magic of our infrastructure is found. With that said, it is a remarkable, innovative, and progressive city. Many in city leadership are concerned about these issues as well as the needs of residents who cannot afford to live in the city center.

Church Planting and Livability

While writing this book, I also have been reading books related to economic development, urban planning, and ministry in various slum communities in Latin America. I was struck by the absurdity of all of this talk about livability in contrast.

I have options. You have options. We have freedom to live almost wherever we want. Again, these are the types of trends that Richard Florida has been pointing out for years. More and more people are simply deciding *where* they want to live before they determine *what* they are going to do to earn a paycheck. Alluring cities with the most urban amenities are on the receiving end of this boom. Livability means a lot. It can make or break a city. In many ways, a city's future rests on its ability to capture and retain young creatives and new start-ups.

But should livability be the determining factor for where we plant new churches? What if we asked that question or applied our logic in the cities of the developing world? That means in places like Lima, Mexico City, Caracas, or Bogotá we would only see new churches planted among the affluent and the shantytowns would be neglected. Is that congruent with the Gospel?

In North America it seems most denominations and church planting organizations "strategically" target the middle-class and above. I am regularly on the websites of all of these entities focusing on planting churches in cities in North America. They seem to only highlight the cool, alluring, and hip parts of the city. It is as though the branding done by cities has been effective not only in attracting new industry, but also in swaying church planters.

Am I being harsh? Yes, but for a reason. Not as an emotional rant or tirade about the mechanisms of denominational life or that of church planting organizations, but to highlight the absurdities of our flawed logic at times in determining where to plant churches. In contrast, "Like a mother who tends most tenderly to the weakest and threatened of her children, so it is with God's care for the poor. And the call of the Gospel is for us to do the same, to make the same option, to show that God's love is universal by focusing our attention on the most threatened among us."[2]

Livability cannot and should not be the overriding determining factor for where we plant new churches. If so, we run the risk of showing partiality. As the writer James says in the Bible:

> My brothers, show no partiality as you hold the faith in our Lord Jesus Christ, the Lord of glory. For if a man wearing a gold ring and fine clothing comes into your assembly, and a poor man in shabby clothing also comes in, and if you pay attention to the one who wears the fine clothing and say, "You sit here in a good place," while you say to the poor man, "You stand over there," or, "Sit down at my feet," have you not then made distinctions among yourselves and become judges

---

[2] Farmer and Gutiérrez, *In the Company of the Poor*, 29.

with evil thoughts? Listen, my beloved brothers, has not God chosen those who are poor in the world to be rich in faith and heirs of the kingdom, which he has promised to those who love him? But you have dishonored the poor man. Are not the rich the ones who oppress you, and the ones who drag you into court? Are they not the ones who blaspheme the honorable name by which you were called?

If you really fulfill the royal law according to the Scripture, "You shall love your neighbor as yourself," you are doing well. But if you show partiality, you are committing sin and are convicted by the law as transgressors.[3]

---

[3] James 2:1-9.

Urban Hinterlands

Chapter 8
Keeping Cities Gritty

So as you can see, I've done a 180-degree turnaround on this topic. I vividly recall pining for years for Tucson's downtown revitalization. Every step forward, whether it was an old building repurposed, talk of a streetcar line, or a new restaurant opening, I became more and more excited. To see a gritty, underused downtown become new was (and is) energizing. However, since those early years of tracking downtown revitalization, I began to see the correlation between livability or desirability and the cost of living. In other words, the uglier the city or neighborhood, the cheaper it is to live there.

Maybe that means our new mission for cities should be to keep them gritty. Could that be a church planting strategy?

Time and distance soften the rough edges of the past. As soon as I start romanticizing Tucson's amazing livability and affordability, all I need to do is go back. It is a jarring reminder that for the most part it is still a gritty and raw city.

But I'm okay with that. There is a good side to that.

Everywhere I go I see Real Estate 101 played out. The nicer the neighborhood, the more expensive the cost of living;

the grittier the neighborhood, the cheaper the cost of living. This is why there often is tension surrounding gentrification. Many "newly livable" neighborhoods were working class or minority neighborhoods. As long as the land and housing weren't deemed valuable or cool, they were left alone. However, as soon as their location or old housing stock became desirable, then what would start off as a trickle of new people moving in would turn into a flood. Gritty becomes fashionable and desirable, and people are priced out of the very neighborhoods they grew up in or have lived in a long time.

Not long ago I took a friend visiting from Montreal to a new wood-oven pizza place along North Williams in inner North/Northeast Portland. As we sat outside, hundreds of cyclists zipped by on their way home. The street scene was vibrant and bustling. There was new construction all up and down the road, mixed-use buildings everywhere. The demographic of everyone we saw was young, White, and really cool. After commenting on our ultra-cool surroundings, I said, "I bet you had no idea that as recent as fifteen years ago this was the heart of the African American community."

If you didn't know, you'd never know.

Another class I teach at Warner Pacific College is Introduction to the City. In the first reflection papers, the topic of gentrification came up repeatedly. Three-quarters of my class are Hispanic or African American. Some grew up watching the neighborhood they love change right before their eyes. Many African Americans felt a sense of loss over a cultural space for the Black community. Yet most of the Hispanic students live east of the 205, which has now become a diverse part of the city and on the receiving end of gentrification.

Not long ago, I signed up to receive email updates and newsletters from an organization in Tucson advocating and promoting livable streets. The Livable Streets Alliance's mission is to "promote healthy communities by empowering people to transform our streets into vibrant places for walking, bicycling, socializing, and play."[1] I'm 100 percent for this as it is needed, especially in a city like Tucson. However, looking forward twenty years (which really isn't that long) my fear is that they may succeed. If that happens, then will the urban core of Tucson still be truly livable?

I like to think that living in Portland is like living in a time warp where we're some future reality that's five, ten, or twenty years down the road. From that vantage point, I can say that we *have* livable streets and our inner-city neighborhoods *are* bikeable and walkable. But for whom? If Tucson succeeds in making its urban core "livable," then my follow-up question is for whom?

I am sure that in the early years the numerous Hispanic neighborhoods and barrios will be included. They will be told about the importance of active transportation and good infrastructure. From bike lanes to complete streets to new fancy bioswales, these neighborhood residents will enjoy a fresh life in the city. However, the more livable a city center or neighborhood becomes, the more it becomes ripe for investment and development. In other words, this will soon

---

[1] Living Streets Alliance. "Welcome to Living Streets Alliance." *Living Streets Alliance.* Online: http://www.livingstreetsalliance.org.

become a magnet for more real estate speculation. Money will begin flowing in. Prices will begin to soar. This will spill to adjacent neighborhoods and alas, you will have a great livable urban core ... for those who can afford it.

Is this what we want?

But what is the alternative?

To keep cities gritty?

In the early 1990s a 158-page report was put out by the City of Portland Bureau of Planning to reflect on the history of the Black community as plans were made to revitalize inner North/Northeast Portland. Titled "The History of Portland's African American Community (1805 to the Present)," it said, "Past redevelopment efforts have taught community planners that preserving social and cultural resources is a key component to any successful revitalization plan."

The painful irony was that seemingly *nothing* was preserved. Inner North/Northeast is no longer a Black community. African Americans have been priced out and displaced. We continue to ignore history and push people aside just to make our cities livable.

We all recognize that unlivable streets, neighborhoods, districts, and city centers are not what we want. The age-old question then becomes how to make cities both livable *and* affordable? I'm not talking about a few token "affordable" units in each new mixed-use building. We have that here in my building and in my neighborhood. Sure, on some level it is helpful, but the reality is that most of those who live in this building could never afford to stay in the building. While they could get away with renting a tiny apartment, they don't have any long-term anchor in the neighborhood. To buy a house is out of the price range of most everyone in this building. Otherwise they wouldn't live here.

From time to time, since living here is a revolving door, we get word that one of our neighbors is moving out to find a cheaper place to live or to actually buy a home. Usually that means they're moving pretty far from the urban core.

Don't get me wrong, I'm enjoying all the new amenities that keep popping up in the neighborhood, from new coffee shops to restaurants to infill which brings more fun vibrancy to the neighborhood. But I've long since given up becoming part of the neighborhood association. I have no long-term investment here. I'll be out soon. An apartment that we looked at in another building just four years ago was $1450 a month. Now? $2300.

The problems are obvious, but what are the solutions?

I don't want this entire book to be reduced to some emotional rant from a disgruntled inner-city renter in Portland. I want to explore how to rectify the problems and to look at what it means to be involved in neighborhoods and cities that are *not* deemed cool or livable? What does it mean or look like to plant churches in the urban hinterlands?

In your city, the urban hinterlands could still be in the heart of the city. Elsewhere, it could be the aging inner-ring suburbs. In either case, how does that context dictate or influence how you go about planting a church? What role would your church play in the dynamics of these neighborhoods and cities? To keep them gritty and uncool? Or to help revitalize and renew them?

Whichever course you take, there are positives and negatives. On the positive front, you could lead the charge to bring in healing, health, wholeness, and essential services and businesses that would bolster the outlook of the community. However, ultimately that then stabilizes the neighborhood, whereby it moves from surviving to thriving, and the cost of living goes up. On the other hand, the positives of leaving the neighborhood gritty, rundown, and uncool is that it continues to be affordable and a landing place for people in need of cheaper housing. But it's not as if that condition is a desired state of permanence. So what do you do? What does a church pastor or planter do in these neighborhoods?

At North Portland Bible College, I teach a course on community development. Ironically, the school sits right in the middle of a transition zone between a gritty neighborhood and a posh hipster neighborhood.

As I rode my scooter up North Williams, I entered a streetscape that as recently as three years ago was drastically different. The single-family detached homes have made way for the four- to six-story mixed-use buildings that now line the streets. It felt as if I were entering an urban canyon hemmed in on both sides. Not Manhattan-like canyons, but still a significant change. Again, if you didn't know the storyline of the neighborhood, you'd really have no idea that only fifteen years ago the majority of people in this part of Portland were African Americans. You see, this urban hinterland has not only become desirable and cool, but increasingly exclusive and pricey. It's not difficult at all to entice new church planters here, but what about today's urban hinterlands that are still gritty and uncool?

Maybe we simply need to leave cities gritty.

I find gritty cities and neighborhoods alluring. They're not polished or pretentious. They simply are. People may not have the time, money, or energy to keep up their yards, but there is still an activity and vibrancy about the area. People are not walled off from one another by affluence. There's a sense of togetherness in a common struggle. It is raw and unfiltered. And it can be refreshing.

Church Planting and Keeping Cities Gritty

Church planters need to know about these changing dynamics of cities. Otherwise, they may actually do more harm than good. New worship gatherings may be launched and small groups implemented, but not planting with an awareness of the story arc of the neighborhood or city is negligence and bad contextualization. It is not loving our new neighbors well.

In our desire to be relevant and plant churches among people like ourselves, we often do so at the expense of people in transitioning urban hinterlands. A neighborhood could be in the midst of transitioning from a minority blue-collar neighborhood into a hotbed for bohemians and other cultural creatives. To many church planters, this is a gold mine for where to plant a new church. This is "cutting edge." But what happens when your church of White twenty-somethings gathers on a Sunday drinking specialty coffee and the surrounding neighborhood is still at least 50 percent blue collar and drinks Folgers? They are watching the neighborhood they grew up in yanked out from under them as housing prices soar. Church planters may talk about "target audiences," but perhaps we should stop and ask, "What is best for the neighborhood?" Or, "What is God's vision for this neighborhood?"

This is where church planters enter the fray of the gentrification debates. It is a paradoxical conversation. On one hand, there is a need to preserve relational ties, community, and the cultural identity that has marked a certain neighborhood or community for decades (or longer). However, at the same time, it is a worn down and tattered neighborhood. More than peeling paint or rusty slides on the playground, but worn in the sense of a growing hopelessness and fatigue from violence, petty crime, declining schools, departing services, and declining businesses.

Church planters are then caught in the paradox of these urban hinterlands. How to be helpful? How not to be harmful?

It is more than making sweeping generalizations like "keep the city or neighborhood gritty" or "let's see revitalization!" Many church planters have never thought about any of these issues. They feel stretched enough by gathering a core group, building up and working towards launching a public gathering, and then growing, shepherding, and leading the new flock. Once in these complex communities, church planters may see for the first time how the impact of context ought to determine (or at least influence) the *how* of church planting.

At times we can be too preoccupied with our weekend gatherings. How should the dynamics of the neighborhood or city shape the role of the church? What happens when the copper mine or paper mill closes? Yes, miners need Jesus, but they also need a job. Loggers need Jesus, but when the mill in town closes, how will they provide for their families when all they know how to do is fell trees or work inside the mill? It is easy to make fun of people who work at Walmart, but what happens when you're an uneducated and unskilled laborer? And then your church full of middle-class environmentally-conscious vegans fight to get that same Walmart closed?

Welcome to the tension. To keep urban hinterlands gritty or not?

Urban Hinterlands

Chapter 9

What Do We Really Want?

Good question. About the time I write off cool cities like Portland or livable and appealing neighborhoods, I am reminded how special they are. And then the other part of me begins thinking about such topics as affordability, access to urban amenities, and the growing economic disparity that has geographic ramifications. Middle-class / white-collar / creative class people live *here* and the working class / service sector live *there*.

What do we really want? What do I really want?

This book is more than a diatribe about struggling with the livability of cities (or the lack thereof). It is ultimately about church planting and ministering in cities or neighborhoods that many have written off. Uncool. Unappealing. Unlivable. Sketchy. *Those* kinds of neighborhoods. This is where we become at odds with ourselves, our feelings, our motives, and our callings.

I find myself in these kinds of conversations on a regular basis as I hang out mostly with church planters. Most often planters simply choose neighborhoods that "fit" and "make sense." More than that, they make decisions on where to plant based upon what they like. The challenge always then becomes what happens when no one likes an unappealing neighborhood?

I'm not calling into question the numerous friends and acquaintances I have who are church planters and their location choices. Many have young families. I hear their worries about local underperforming schools and wanting to make sure they put their kids in good schools in a solid school district. I listen as they talk about living in safe neighborhoods. I hear those kinds of conversations and many more like them.

This reinforces my ideas and theories about why we don't plant churches in gritty neighborhoods. Too much personal cost and sacrifice.

Ouch.

Did I just really say that out loud?

Yesterday I showed my gentrification class at Warner Pacific College a short video about gentrification in Harlem, including Black-on-Black gentrification. In the video, the two main figures being interviewed, both African American, talked about the divide even among the incoming middle-class, white-collar Blacks versus the working-class Blacks who have called the neighborhood home for a long time. One of the scenes that stood out was footage of Harlem in the 1980s. It looked like London when it was bombed during WWII.

It is probably safe to say that church planters were not flocking to Harlem back then to plant cool churches. That is not to say churches were not being started or that God was not at work. But it is an extreme example of changing urban neighborhoods where church planters typically fear to tread. Add into the mix that many church planters have young families and all of a sudden life and church planting become more complicated.

How comfortable are we with sacrificing? Is our Americanized version of the Gospel leading us to simply plant in safe and trendy neighborhoods?

I get it. These are tough questions, but we should be asking tough questions. Just like we should be having tough conversations about race, our faith, the church, and how all of these ought to be seen through the lens of the Gospel. One thing I appreciate about the classes I teach, since they all get into gentrification, race, racism, and inequality, is that there is permission to *just talk*. I have Hispanic, Latino, African, African-American, Asian, and Caucasian students, but we can have honest and frank conversations as we process these things together.

I want this book to be like that in a way for church planters. To provide a platform to talk about the obvious. But sometimes we feel scandalized to talk about the obvious. In no way am I here to browbeat you or to guilt you. I simply want to have an honest conversation and ask blunt questions. Not to shame, but to stir. To drive us deeper into our callings and to peel back the enculturated layers of the Gospel in our context.

So then what do we really want?

My intention in writing this book is to begin shifting our attention toward uncool neighborhoods and cities. Plain and simple. Besides, all of the cool urban neighborhoods and alluring suburbs won't have any difficulty attracting new church planters. That's already happening and already has happened.

Last weekend I led a studio on exegeting the city in Claremont, a suburb of Los Angeles. "Suburb" is a stretch since it was and is its own town / city that eventually was swallowed up by sprawl. But its roots and foundation go back to the late 1800s, along with its numerous colleges.

As I walked the downtown (or the "Village") with a church planter, we talked about all things cities and urban church planting. The perception he had is that I'm about all things "urban" or "inner-city." I stopped and explained that indeed for a long while I was (and still am) fascinated about such topics as urban renewal, gentrification, and population inversion, but more and more (with this book in mind) I said my attention and affection have shifted to uncool neighborhoods and cities. In other words, I'm more interested in seeing new churches planted in uncool places like Pomona rather than another hipster church plant in downtown LA.

Now don't confuse this change of affections with a disdain for planting churches in urban neighborhoods. I'm 100 percent for that. What I am saying is that alongside of planting churches *there* (cool) I want us to think and consider planting churches *here* (uncool). Are you with me?

So what is it that we really want?

We all naturally seek comfort. For a moment I want you to forget everything I've written. There is something innate within us that compels us to seek safety, comfort, familiarity, security, and peace. We are protective of ourselves and our families. This is quite natural and normative. I am not too sure why or how this works, but it just does. We are drawn to certain places and experiences more than others. There is some kind of gravitational pull toward what is beautiful, alluring, safe, comforting, and pleasant.

Yesterday I spent part of the morning with my brother-in-law Caleb and son Seth walking around Northwest Portland in the Alphabet District along NW 23rd. It is a vibrant street scene with lots of happy pedestrians strolling from shop to shop and from cafe to cafe. We stopped at a hipster donut shop and then went over to a hipster coffee shop. Everything was over-the-top cool. The people were all well-dressed and beautiful. Now, why is this so appealing?

I could let my guard down. I could breathe easy. No need to put my "street face" on. We chatted with people, petted dogs, and had a great time. I'm naturally drawn to places like these.

But the Gospel is countercultural and counterintuitive.

As God through the death, burial, and resurrection of Christ breathes new life into us, he makes us a new creation. His Spirit indwells us and not only are we transformed but that transformation process begins rearranging everything in our lives. We are compelled. We are compelled to sacrifice, to seek the welfare of our cities and others, to risk, and to take leaps of faith. Our lives are no longer about seeking our own glory or pleasure, but yet ironically we encounter deep and more fulfilling pleasure, experiences, and meaning because of our identity in Christ. We are given a greater capacity to enjoy our lives and relationships. We are grounded and rooted in Christ.

This is where it is all paradoxical. Because of the Gospel, we give our lives away and yet at the same time we burrow deeper into loving and leading our families. This is the center stage of the drama of this book and where the tension is. On the one hand we joyfully sacrifice for the Gospel, and on the other we are stewards of the families that God has blessed us with.

When our sole focus is on sacrifice, we can run the risk of leading our families poorly and neglecting their needs. But when our sole focus is on our families, we never sacrifice for the Gospel. How do we do both? Where is the happy middle ground? This "location" then is the focal point of this book.

Do we seek out cool neighborhoods knowing our families will have an enjoyable time and are safe and comfortable? Or do we seek out an uncool (troubled) neighborhood where the schools may be lousy and it is not the safest place?

The Gospel for the Urban Hinterlands

We have a lot of terms that accompany our initial transformation when we are confronted with the Gospel. After our transition from darkness to light we begin to grow. We have a number of names for it. Spiritual growth and maturity. Sanctification. Discipleship. Transformation.

In Chapter 3, I introduced to you the idea of conversion as spelled out in the book *In the Company of the Poor*. More than what happens upon the moment we are born anew in Christ, the term, synonymous with sanctification or spiritual growth, describes an ongoing, continual process. What is noteworthy in the book, though, are the parameters or boundaries of this conversion. As Western evangelicals we primarily focus on what happens *internally*. In other words, much talk about spiritual growth revolves around character development, stopping sinful habits and patterns, and day-by-day renewing the inner man. However, more is at stake in our conversion. Gutiérrez writes:

> The change called for is not simply an interior one but one that involves the entire person as a corporeal being (a factor of human solidarity) and therefore also has consequences for the web of social relationships of which the individual is a part. That is why Archbishop Romero could make this strong statement: 'Nowadays an authentic Christian conversion must lead to an unmasking of the social mechanisms that turn the worker and the peasant into marginalized persons. Why do the rural poor become part of society only in the coffee- and cotton-picking seasons?' The will to conversion should lead to this kind of concrete analysis.[1]

This sounds strikingly familiar to what the biblical writer James was alluding to when he wrote, "But someone will say, 'You have faith and I have works.' Show me your faith apart from your works, and I will show you my faith by my works."[2] It is not that good works saves us, but that our conversion is demonstrated by our outer lives.

When it comes to the urban hinterlands, what do we really want? I would say that all of the church planters that I know want one thing: to live a life giving glory to God and to point sinners to the cross. With that said, I know I need more areas of my life radically converted. From darkness to light. From sinful negligence to holy embrace. "The encounter with

---

[1] Farmer and Gutiérrez, *In the Company of the Poor*, 74-75.

[2] James 2:18.

the Lord in the inmost recesses of the individual does not exclude but rather calls for a similar encounter in the depths of the wretchedness in which the poor of our countries live."[3]

What we want may not always be what we need. I like safety, comfort, routine, and familiarity. Not very many of us run directly into the path of hardship or adversity. And yet, that is the only thing in life that causes spiritual growth and maturity. We seemingly only grow in the face of discomfort. This pain and struggle is what the Lord then uses in our lives to grow and mature us. While it is tempting to seek comfort, safety, and familiarity, more of us need to eschew that. I'm not talking about being impulsive, reckless, and foolish. Instead we need to let the Gospel so radically alter our values, identity, and life goals that we would find ourselves seeking out the urban hinterlands.

Because Christ died for the people there, too. He gave it all up to be bruised and battered on our behalf. As a result, our sacrifice of comfort pales in comparison.

---

[3] Farmer and Gutiérrez, *In the Company of the Poor*, 75.

Chapter 10

Loving Uncool Places

I shared in the last chapter that since I'm viewed as the "city" guy many have told me they assume I'm into renewed city centers, urban church planting, downtowns, the in-migration of the creative class, and trendy revitalized (gentrified) neighborhoods and districts, which is entirely true. The last few years those are the topics I have focused on. I am curious about the trends reshaping urban America and how that plays out in the built environment, urban mobility (transportation), and the rise of the knowledge-based (or artisan or creative) economies. In other words, this perception is true, somewhat.

But really my heart is for the off-the-beaten-paths kinds of places. I'm like that guy who falls in love with a band when they are obscure and playing in front of twelve people in a rundown dive bar. When the band gets big, I move on to another band. I did love all things downtown and inner-city when we weren't really talking about it or planting churches there. I was one of the people loudly beating the drum to call us back into the urban core to plant churches.

But now we're planting in the city. The city is the hotspot to plant churches. That obscure band is now opening up for U2 or Coldplay. So I've begun moving on, so to speak, to the next underdog who needs an advocate.

That has been part of my angst as I've been writing this book. It is rather scandalous for me to admit that I'm not really interested in urban cores any longer, especially when all of my previous books have been narrowly focused on church planting, bicycles, gentrification, and mobility in the heart of the city. This past weekend it finally clicked for me. The transition has been complete. I'm over the inner city. My obscure band signed a record deal with a major label.

Last weekend I led a couple of breakout sessions at a church planting conference in Colorado Springs. It was a fun time connecting with planters and others involved in church planting. The focus of my presentations and discussions revolved around how urban form shapes church planting as well as church planting in complex urban contexts. It was a special time interacting with leaders, but I noticed I was especially drawn when I heard of people planting churches in uncool neighborhoods and cities. This helps me understand why I *loved* ministering in Tucson and since moving to Portland I feel like I've been dying a thousand deaths: the city's so cool that everyone knows it. I'm not.

It is beyond easy to get church planters to LoDo in Denver or the inner-city in Portland, but how about Pueblo, Colorado? No one goes to Pueblo to plant. It's just not that cool.

I spent a lot of time in each of my sessions talking about the geography of church planting and site selection for new church plants. It's that same adage that I've been saying repeatedly the last few years: the trendier the neighborhood district or city, the more church planters flock there. In other words, you don't need to actively recruit planters to LoDo or the Pearl since they are already coming in droves. But to get church planters to Ontario, Oregon, or Pueblo, Colorado, or Las Cruces, New Mexico? Good luck.

If we want to plant churches in neighborhoods and cities that we want to live in, then where does that leave uncool places? How do we love uncool places? Here are some starting points:

1. Move there.
2. Fall in love with the city and people "as is."
3. Find out what makes that place special.
4. Invite others to move there with you.
5. When you move there don't try to make it cool.
6. See why God finds this place special.

Easy, right?

Here's my new proposal for where we need to focus our efforts on church planting. Simply Google "the worst cities in America" (or wherever), and begin there. Seriously. This could be the list of the ugliest cities or those with the most crime, but begin searching. Unfortunately there is a lot of debate (which I think is absurd) out there about which cities are the worst or the ugliest. One website listed New York City and Las Vegas as some of the worst or ugliest cities. I disagree.

So what are the ugly and non-sexy cities? I can think of scores out West from Bakersfield, California, to Tucson, Arizona, to Reno, Nevada, to Yuma, Arizona, for starters.

Then there are hundreds of smaller cities that are completely off the radar of anyone involved in church planting. These are the Pueblos of the world. Good luck hearing anyone emphasizing the need to plant churches in places like that.

Surprisingly in one of my sessions there was a woman who was actually part of a core team looking to plant a church in Pueblo. Rightly so she asked me what I thought of the many denominations and networks whose exclusive focus is on "alpha cities" or "top-tiered cities" (or however we want to describe it). Many of these church planting entities have put all of their eggs in the baskets of these cities. Many have channeled funding to give priority to church planters there. So where does that leave uncool lesser cities?

Truth be told, as I've argued throughout this book, in each of these top-tiered urban centers there are uncool, unappealing, and uninviting neighborhoods, districts, and parts of the city. Since we focus on significant cities (however we define that) and trending "influential" neighborhoods, that means we avert our attention from what we deem "lesser" places.

There is an assumption that we should spend all of our time, efforts, and money going after the "power brokers" or "change agents" in the city. But with the paradoxical nature of the Gospel and how God has worked throughout history, we may need to rethink that one. If not, we run the risk of doing what James wrote in his epistle, showing partiality.

Who are you really? Who am I really? I know I'm just a simple kid who grew up in obscurity in small-town Iowa. No off-the-charts gifts, talents, or abilities. Nothing pause-worthy. Just plain. Average. Maybe I "get" uncool because I grew up uncool in an uncool town in an uncool state.

However, how are we to really love uncool places?

That question really is at the crux of this book and its scope. How do we not only love uncool places, but search them out and plant our lives, the Gospel, and churches there?

Loving Uncool Places

In the first few chapters, I detailed my transition from Tucson to Portland as well as some of the motivating factors behind it. In many ways, I did exactly the *opposite* of what I have been advocating throughout this book. Guilty as charged.

But we most often learn from our failures and shortcomings.

Not that moving to Portland was a failure, by any stretch. I've been able to do more and experience more in terms of my calling, wiring, and gifting than I could have in Tucson. But that decision still haunts me. There is still a magnetic draw and appeal that the Lord may use in my life someday. But for the foreseeable future, Portland is my home.

I would venture to say that most of you don't live in a city like Portland. Maybe you battle with some of the identity and image issues that come from where you live. That's why this book is for you. Not in some sort of feeling sorry kind of way, but to encourage, help, and prod you to lean into your city more and love it more fully and deeply. I want that for you. Your city needs you. The Gospel compels you.

I've been rereading my journal entries from the year 2003 when we first landed in Tucson. Again, it was a city I didn't understand or like. However, as I read back through my journal entries leading up to launch, there is a common theme of crying out before the Lord on behalf of lost people in the city. It had nothing to do with how cool or uncool the city was. I was compelled to go and plant the Gospel. May that calling never escape my attention or focus regardless of where I live. And may the same be true for you.

Afterword

My heart yearns to see churches planted in the off-the-beaten-path kinds of places, whether urban or suburban neighborhoods, lower-tiered cities, or other smaller cities. Am I then over the inner-city in North America? Not completely. I'm drawn to the life and culture that urban density offers. However, what has changed is the emphasis or locus of mission for me. My first and foremost desire is to see churches planted in under-reached areas. Maybe in Portland that means in the low-density sprawl east of the 205 but in other places like La Paz, Bolivia, it is in the high-density urban core.

I hope I have stirred the waters to get you thinking more deeply about the Gospel, church planting, and cities.

Bibliography

Angus Reid Institute. "Lotusland Blues: One-In-Five Metro
    Vancouverites Experience Extreme Housing & Traffic
    Pain; Most of Them Think of Leaving." *Angus Reid
    Institute*. Online: http://angusreid.org/vancouver-real-
    estate/.
Bishop, Bill. *The Big Sort: Why the Clustering of Like-Minded
    America is Tearing Us Apart*. New York: Houghton
    Mifflin, 2008.
Farmer, Paul and Gustavo Gutierrez. *In the Company of the
    Poor: Conversations with Dr. Paul Farmer and Fr. Gustavo
    Gutierrez*. Mayknoll: Orbis, 2013.
Hurst, Tyler. "Why My Apartment is Good for Portland."
    Willamette Weekly, June 9, 2015. Online: http://
    www.wweek.com/portland/article-24869-
    why_my_apartment_is_good_for_portland.html.
International Making Cities Livable. "The Value of Rankings
    and the Meaning of Livability." *International Making
    Cities Livable*. Online: http://www.livablecities.org/blog/
    value-rankings-and-meaning-livability.
Keller, Timothy. *The Prodigal God: Recovering the Heart of the
    Christian Faith*. New York: Riverhead, 2008.
Manning, Jeff. "Working Class Priced Out, Kicked Out In
    New Portland Housing Boom." *The Oregonian*, September
    22, 2015. Online: http://www.oregonlive.com/watchdog/
    index.ssf/2015/09/post_19.html.
Schuurman, Douglas J. *Vocation: Discerning Our Callings in
    Life*. Grand Rapids: Eerdmans, 2004.
UN-Habitat, *Planning Sustainable Cities: Global Report on
    Human Settlements 2009*. London: Earthscan, 2009.

About the Author

Coffee and bicycles define Sean's urban existence. He believes the best way to explore cities is on the seat of a bicycle or hanging out in third-wave coffee shops. Sean works for The Evangelical Alliance Mission (TEAM.org) as a Church Planting Strategist.

www.seanbenesh.net

Made in the USA
Coppell, TX
03 September 2021

61717725R00066